BIGGER DREAMS

A Two Act Play about Deaf Politician Gary Malkowski

By Richard Medugno

ISBN: 1-4107-2536-7 (e-book)
ISBN: 1-4107-2537-5 (Paperback)

Library of Congress Control Number: 2003092657

This book is printed on acid free paper.

Printed in the United States of America
Bloomington, IN

1stBooks – rev. 04/30/03

CAST LIST

There are 32 roles if a separate actor is cast for each role, however, the play is written with the idea that a chorus of 8-12 deaf, hard-of-hearing and hearing actors and actresses would play two or three roles each.

Deaf & Hard-of-hearing Characters:
Gary Malkowski, 30-45
Young Gary, 16-18
James Tucker, 30-45, Gary's friend from Gallaudet
Patty Shores-Hermann, 30-45, Gary's friend from Gallaudet
Mary Malkowski, 30-45, Gary's first wife
Student, 20-25, Gary's client
Gallaudet Students, 20-25, Gary's classmates
Protesters & Supporters, various, for group scenes
TV Camera Operator, 25-40, works with TV reporters

Hearing Characters who Speak and Sign:
Narrator, 30-50
Karen, 30-40, Gary's second wife
Linda, 35-50, Gary's sister
Mark Bulligan, 25-45, Gary's high school teacher
Mary Lamont, 25-50, Gary's high school teacher
Judy Rebeck, 35-50, colleague from the Canadian Hearing Society
Iris Boshes, 35-50, colleague from the Canadian Hearing Society
Denis Morrice, 40-60. colleague from the Canadian Hearing Society
Dean Will, 30-40, a sign language interpreter

<u>Hearing Characters Who Don't Sign:</u>
Cecile Malkowski, 55-70, Gary's mother
Bob Malkowski, 55-70, Gary's father
Truck Driver, 25-55, neighbor
Joey, 12-16, neighbor
Secretary #1, 30-60, employee of Ministry of Education
Secretary #2, 30-60, employee of Ministry of Education
Richard Johnston, 40-60, Member of Provincial Parliament
Reporter #1, 25-55, member of the Toronto media
Reporter #2, 25-55, member of the Toronto media
Bob Rae, 35-45, leader of the New Democratic Party
Marcia McVea, 35-50, Gary's campaign manager
Woman, 35-60, East York resident
Senior Citizen, 60-70, East York resident
Christine Hart, 40-50, Member of Provincial Parliament
George Bryson, 40-60, Conservative candidate

Playwright's Notes about the script of BIGGER DREAMS:

1) Dialogue that is expressed in sign language only, where there is no voice interpretation by a character/actor, is indicated in the script in all caps. Voice interpreting for hearing audience members can be provided through the theatre's P.A. system.

2) When dialogue is written with two names, in most cases GARY & JUDY or GARY & DEAN, the first character is the signer and the second is voice interpreting the signer's signs.

3) Throughout most of the play, when hearing, non-signing characters are speaking and a character is not interpreting, an ASL interpreter should be upstage of the actor.

Playwright's Notes about the staging of BIGGER DREAMS:

Probably the best way to stage this play is with an open setting that has different levels, set pieces and props that can be easily adapted to symbolize different locales. Lighting will be a key element to identify changes in scene and passage of time. I envision all the actors being on stage throughout the course of the play, perhaps sitting on stools when not involved in a scene. As most productions will opt for having a chorus of actors performing the many small roles, actors with multiple parts may want to help differentiate the characters they play with costume (hats and/or accessories) and personal props.

Dedication:

For Carlee, Sara, Marissa, Christopher, Lukas, Jesse, Terence and, especially Miranda

PROLOGUE

Lights up. A spotlight picks up the NARRATOR, *a man in his 30's, wearing a coat and tie. He stands center stage. He speaks and signs at the same time.*

NARRATOR:

I met Gary Malkowski in1993 in Ontario, Canada. We lived on the same street in East York, a borough of Metropolitan Toronto. At the time, I had a two-year-old daughter, who was born profoundly deaf. My wife and I had just found this out a few months earlier.

We started learning sign language soon after that. A local organization put us in touch with a deaf family and they came to our home to visit. We began to learn that there was a Deaf culture and that Deaf people were quite happy being who and how they were. They did not consider deafness a disability. It was intriguing to us. It sounded like a great approach if one wanted a child to be psychologically well-balanced and have good self-esteem.

We enrolled our daughter in a special pre-school for deaf children and the hearing children of Deaf parents.

When Gary Malkowski parked his car in front of our house one morning, I didn't know what to expect. He was here to carpool my daughter and his son to the pre-school. I walked my daughter down the driveway as Gary jumped out of his car and said...

A spotlight comes up on GARY. *He is wearing a suit and tie. He has a full beard and a bald head.*

> GARY
> (*Voicing and signing.*)

Good morning.
> (*Signing and mouthing only.*)
MUST BE STRANGE TO HAVE YOUR M.P.P.
DRIVING YOUR DAUGHTER TO SCHOOL.

> NARRATOR
> (*To the audience.*)

I just stared at him. I didn't have a clue to what he was trying to say to me.

> GARY

MUST BE STRANGE TO HAVE YOUR M.P.P.
DRIVING YOUR DAUGHTER TO SCHOOL.

> NARRATOR

Again, I didn't understand. But I did know the sign for repeat. (*Signing.*) REPEAT, PLEASE.

> GARY

MUST BE STRANGE TO HAVE YOUR M.P.P.
DRIVING YOUR DAUGHTER TO SCHOOL.

> NARRATOR

SORRY. REPEAT.

> GARY
> (*Voicing as he signs.*)

MUST BE STRANGE TO HAVE YOUR M.P.P.
DRIVING YOUR DAUGHTER TO SCHOOL.

NARRATOR

Again, please....(*As* GARY *signs the same sentence*.) Must be something to have my M.P.P. driving my daughter to school. What's...? (*Signing "STRANGE".*)

GARY
(Voicing and signing "STRANGE.")

Shrang. Shrang. Shrang.

NARRATOR

I stood there shaking my head like an idiot. (*Signing and voicing*.)
Sorry, I don't understand.

GARY
(Fingerspells.)

S-T-R-A-N-G-E.

NARRATOR
(Totally confused.)

String? It must be string? (*Fingerspelling*.) S-T-R-I-N-G?

GARY
(Shaking his head.)

NO! S-T-R-A-N-G-E.

NARRATOR
(To the audience.)

I still didn't get it. I was particularly dense that morning. Finally, Gary got me to understand. (*To* GARY, *signing*.) I don't understand.

3

> GARY
> (*Fingerspelling.*)

O-D-D.

> NARRATOR

O-D-D. Odd! Oh, odd! You meant strange!

> GARY
> (*Smiling broadly and nodding.*)

Shrang!

> NARRATOR

It must be strange to have my M.P.P. driving my daughter to school.

> GARY
> *(Laughing.)*

PAH!

> NARRATOR
> *(Laughing.)*

You're my M.P.P.?! You're a politician?!

> GARY

YES. SEE YA LATER.

> NARRATOR

I just stood there and watched as he drove off with our kids and thought, "How in the hell did a deaf guy become a Member of the Provincial Parliament of Ontario?" This is when my dreams for my daughter began to grow.

Lights out.

ACT ONE

A spotlight on a door frame and a closed door. CECILE, *a woman of 35 years wearing an apron, walks into the light. She speaks to the audience with a French-Canadian accent.*

CECILE
(*To the audience.*)

Gary was a sickly child. He was born pre-mature. At first, we didn't think anything was wrong with him. Then I started to think something was wrong, but I couldn't put my finger on it. I kept taking him to the family doctor and saying, "There's something wrong with him". And the doctor kept saying, "No, there's nothing wrong with him."

There is a loud knock at the door. CECILE *opens the door revealing a* TRUCK DRIVER.

CECILE
Yes?

TRUCK DRIVER
Excuse me, ma'am. Is that your boy out there?

CECILE
No. My boy's out back---
(*Looking again.*)

Wait a minute...That is him. He must have sneaked out the side gate. Gary! Gary, get outta the street! Linda, get your brother out of the street!

TRUCK DRIVER
Ma'am, I think you boy's deaf.

5

CECILE

No! What are you talking about? He can't be.

TRUCK DRIVER

I really think so. You just yelled at him and he didn't even turn to look. And I was blasting my truck horn and he never moved. He just stood there with his back to the truck. I'd take him to the doctor, if he were my son.

CECILE

Yes, maybe I should....Thank you.

She closes the door.

CECILE
(*To the audience.*)

I did what the truck driver said. I took Gary to the doctor's again. Only this time we went to an ear, nose and throat specialist. They told me when I got there to carry Gary with his back to the doctor. So, I was talking to the doctor and he said, 'If he's not deaf, he's pretty close to it.' They put Gary on all these machines and tested him. They said he had a bit of hearing, but not much. So, they removed his tonsils and adenoids. He had a lot of trouble with colds. They thought that might help. It didn't help much.

(She sighs.)

There wasn't much help for us in those days. They just told us to write the John Tracy Clinic in California. They sent us some things to do with Gary. We were just blue-collar people, living in the east end of Hamilton, Ontario, a steel town. We didn't have any idea what to do. We found out that

Hamilton had a special pre-school for deaf, so we just started to send him there. Grace Harris was the teacher. Everybody said she was a wonderful teacher of the deaf. But I didn't like her.

GRACE HARRIS
(*Appearing in a spot downstage. Speaks rather haughtily.*)

Gary's speech has not developed to any notable extent. Occasionally, he says a whole word quite clearly and parts of other words with meaning. Usually, this is in play situations when he is off guard. At least we are certain that he is absorbing language meanings and is capable of learning to understand language and to speak. It is taking him some time to become adjusted to changes and to group associations. He pays good attention in speech training lessons, even though his responses are not frequent. He will continue to need consistent training in speech and lipreading.
(*Lights out on* GRACE.)

GARY
(*Appearing in a spotlight upstage of his mother.*)

NATURALLY, IT WAS DIFFICULT FOR MY PARENTS TO ACCEPT MY 'HANDICAP', ESPECIALLY MY FATHER. THIS WAS BECAUSE THEY WERE VERY CONCERNED ABOUT MY EDUCATION. THEY WERE PLACED IN AN AWKWARD POSITION HAVING TO COPE WITH A PRELINGUALLY AND PROFOUNDLY DEAF CHILD. COMMUNICATING WITH A DEAF CHILD WAS A NEW AND FRUSTRATING EXPERIENCE FOR THEM...I DON'T

7

REMEMBER MUCH ABOUT THAT ORAL
SCHOOL, EXCEPT THAT THEY WOULD SLAP
YOUR HANDS IF YOU TRIED TO SIGN.

WHEN I WAS FIVE YEARS OLD, I BECAME A
RESIDENT STUDENT AT THE ONTARIO
SCHOOL FOR THE DEAF IN MILTON,
ONTARIO, ABOUT A HALF-HOUR DRIVE
FROM MY HOMETOWN OF HAMILTON.
WHEN I WAS SENT THERE, I SUFFERED
SOME TRAUMA FROM SEPARATION FROM
MY FAMILY.   IT WAS FRIGHTENING
BECAUSE OF THE SIZE OF THE
INSTITUTION, THE LARGE NUMBER OF
UNRELATED AND UNFAMILIAR ADULTS
AND CHILDREN WHO LIVED TOGETHER. IT
WAS VERY DIFFERENT FROM FAMILY
LIVING.   I WAS VERY ANGRY AT MY
PARENTS AS I THOUGHT THEY LEFT ME
FOR GOOD. BUT THEY DID COME BACK
AND PICK ME UP. I SOON LEARNED THAT I
WOULD STAY IN THE DORMS DURING THE
WEEK AND GO HOME ON THE WEEKENDS.
OH, I LOVED IT. THE CULTURE AND THE
LANGUAGE AND THE COMMUNICATION
WITH MY PEERS, THE SENSE OF
TOGETHERNESS.   WE COULDN'T SIGN
DURING THE CLASS TIME, BUT DURING
RECESS AND AFTER SCHOOL WE COULD. I
DIDN'T FEEL LONELY. I CHERISHED MY
YEARS IN SCHOOL.

YOU KNOW, IT GOT TO THE POINT WHERE I
DIDN'T WANT TO GO HOME ON WEEKENDS
BECAUSE IN THE DORMS I COULD REALLY
COMMUNICATE WITH PEOPLE. I GOT MOST

OF MY EDUCATION OUTSIDE THE CLASSROOM.

Spotlight comes up on LINDA who is upstage of GARY.

LINDA
(*Signing and speaking.*)
Gary was spoiled rotten. When he came home from school he got all kinds of attention and special treats. Resentment and communication difficulties prevented him from really bonding with us---his brothers and sisters.

But Gary was a happy-go-lucky kid. He was a clown, always putting on a show. To communicate he would mime and gesture. But he was ostracized when he was not entertaining the neighborhood kids. They didn't have the patience for him.

Lights out on LINDA.

GARY

AT HOME, MY PARENTS TRIED TO COMMUNICATE WITH ME THROUGH THE ORAL METHOD, BUT I COULDN'T UNDERSTAND THEM MOST OF THE TIME. THAT INCREASED THEIR FRUSTRATION. MY FATHER WAS IMPATIENT AND STUBBORN. MY MOTHER LOST HER TEMPER EASILY. IT WAS DIFFICULT FOR ME TO COPE. WHEN I WAS EIGHT YEARS OLD, I ASKED THEM TO ALLOW ME TO JOIN LITTLE LEAGUE HOCKEY. THEY SAID, 'NO, YOU CAN'T PLAY, YOU CAN'T HEAR.' I WAS VERY DEPPRESSED BECAUSE I DIDN'T HAVE AN OPPORTUNITY TO JOIN AND TO

COMMUNICATE WELL WITH HEARING
PEOPLE. AS I GREW OLDER, MY
RELATIONSHIP WITH MY PARENTS
BECAME MORE UPSETTING...(*Smiles.*) LIKE
ALL TEENAGERS AND THEIR PARENTS.....I
REMEMBER ONE TIME...HOW WOULD YOU
FEEL IF YOUR FATHER ASKED A NEIGHBOR
BOY TO HELP HIM PAINT YOUR GARAGE
INSTEAD OF YOU?

*Lights cross fade to: outside of the Malkowskis' garage. A
ladder leans against a wall.* YOUNG GARY, *a teenager
with stringy, long hair, is dribbling a basketball.*

Enters BOB, *a small but stocky older man with closely
cropped gray hair. He is dressed in janitor's overalls. He
carries an open can of paint.* JOEY, *a young kid, the same
age as* YOUNG GARY, *follows closely behind* BOB *with
paintbrushes.*

YOUNG GARY

(*Signs or gestures.*)

WHAT'S UP?

BOB

(*With a distinct Polish accent,
waving him away.*)

You get out of here.

YOUNG GARY

(To JOEY, *voicing and signing.*)

What doing?

JOEY

Your father asked me to help him.

10

YOUNG GARY

WHY?!
>   (JOEY *shrugs. He turns to* BOB.)
Papa? Why not me?

BOB

You are no help to me. Go play ball in the front.
Come here, Joey. You hand the bucket to me when
I get up there.

BOB *puts down the can of paint and climbs up the ladder to
the roof.* YOUNG GARY *looks at* JOEY *with anger and
hurt in his eyes.* JOEY *shrugs.* BOB, *on the roof, walks out
of sight.*

JOEY

He said he would give me five bucks.

JOEY *picks up the can of paint and starts up the ladder.*
YOUNG GARY *angrily throws the ball at* JOEY, *just
missing him. Suddenly, he rushes to the ladder and begins
to shake it violently.* JOEY, *who is trying to balance the
can of paint and hang on to the ladder, starts yelling.*

JOEY

No! No! Gary, no!
(YOUNG GARY *keeps shaking the ladder.*)
Bob! Bob!

BOB
(Re-appearing.)
What the hell?!

Suddenly, the can of paint goes flying offstage as JOEY *needs both hands to hold onto the ladder. For a second, there is silence as all three look off to see the paint splatter.* BOB *grabs his head between both hands and yells "Ugh!" or something in Polish.*

GARY
(*To* JOEY.)

Go home!

JOEY
(*Scrambling down the ladder.*)

He's going to kill you!

BOB
(*Point his finger at* YOUNG GARY.)

I'm going to kill you, you son-of-a-bitch!

YOUNG GARY *mimics his father as* JOEY *races off.* BOB *starts for the ladder, but* YOUNG GARY *gets to it first and pulls it away from the roof.* BOB *gets one hand on the last rung. There is a brief tug-of-war, before* YOUNG GARY *using the leverage he has from being on the ground, wrests it free.*

BOB

Come back with that! Gary! Gary!

YOUNG GARY *takes the ladder and throws it offstage.*

BOB

Cecile! Cecile!

YOUNG GARY *looks up at his father and laughs.*

BOB
(*Threatening with his finger.*)
Bring back that ladder right now!

YOUNG GARY
(*Voicing.*)
Shut up, you dumb Pollock!

BOB *is struck dumb. He just stares at* YOUNG GARY.

YOUNG GARY
(*Waving.*)
Bye, bye.

YOUNG GARY *runs off, laughing. Lights slowly fade on* BOB *as he starts to yell.*

BOB
(*Boiling mad.*)
Cecile! Cecile!! AHHHHHHH!

Spotlight comes back up on GARY, *who is chuckling as he witnesses the memory ending.*

GARY
MY FATHER AND I DIDN'T GET ALONG. IT WAS A DIFFICULT RELATIONSHIP. I KNEW HOW TO BOTHER MY FATHER. HE CAME TO CANADA AFTER WORLD WAR TWO. HE WAS A POLISH SOLDIER WHO WAS FORCED TO FIGHT WITH THE GERMAN ARMY. I USED TO SAY HE WAS A NAZI. OH, BOY...(*Laughing.*) HE WOULD GET SO MAD AT ME....I REMEMBER ANOTHER TIME

WHEN I WAS PLAYING STREET HOCKEY
WITH SOME FRIENDS IN THE DAIRY QUEEN
PARKING LOT....

Lights up on a bare stage with YOUNG GARY *and* JOEY
*and two other young men with hockey-sticks and a plastic
"whiffle" ball. They are playing two-on-two street hockey
and having a good time. After a few moments,* BOB
MALKOWSKI *enters from offstage.*

He just stands there looking annoyed. YOUNG GARY *has
his back to his father.* JOEY *notices* BOB *first and
immediately stops playing.*

> JOEY

Hi, Bob.

BOB *nods and the others stop.* YOUNG GARY *turns to
see his father.*

> YOUNG GARY
> (*Signing, speaking and then
> smiling.*)

Hello, old man!

BOB *points to his watch.* YOUNG GARY *shrugs and
gestures, "So?"*

> BOB
> (*Gesturing eating food.*)

It's dinner time.

> YOUNG GARY
> (*Shaking his head and making a
> face.*)

I'M NOT HUNGRY.

14

BOB
(*Waving him over.*)

Come on, let's go!

YOUNG GARY
(*Shaking his head and voicing.*)

No.

BOB
(*Angrily.*)

What? What'd you say to me?

The other boys start to move to the periphery of the scene. Afraid.

YOUNG GARY
(*With a lot of attitude.*)

YOU DEAF? I SAID 'NO!'

BOB
(*Reaching for his belt.*)

Why you son-of-a-bitch!

JOEY
(*Coming down to* YOUNG GARY, *trying to push him off.*)

Gary, just go.

YOUNG GARY
(*Boasting to his friends.*)

I'M NOT AFRAID OF HIM.

BOB *whips off his belt and begins to threaten* YOUNG GARY *with it.* YOUNG GARY *looks and just laughs.*

BOB *starts swing the belt with the buckle at the end and moving in* YOUNG GARY's *direction.*

> YOUNG GARY
> (*Brandishing his hockey stick.*)

COME ON! COME ON!

> JOEY
> (*Rushing to the periphery again.*)

Oh, shit!

BOB *continues to move in* YOUNG GARY's *direction.* YOUNG GARY *holds his ground and begins to jab at this father with the hockey stick.* BOB's *anger gets the best of him and he chases* YOUNG GARY *around in circles, swinging his belt.* YOUNG GARY *fends him off with the hockey stick, laughing each time his father's attempt to reach him fails. Soon his friends are no longer afraid and join in on the laughter. Finally,* BOB *loses his belt when it wraps around the hockey stick and* YOUNG GARY *jerks it from his father's hands.*

> YOUNG GARY
> (*Brandishing the belt and voicing.*)

I win!

> BOB
> (*Red-faced and exhausted.*)

You son-of-a-bitch!....

> YOUNG GARY
> (*Waving and voicing.*)

Bye-Bye, Papa.

YOUNG GARY *runs off, "high-fiving" his three friends as he goes.* BOB *follows his son slowly off, threatening with his raised fist as he exits.*

Lights cross-fade from scene and a spotlight comes back on GARY.

> GARY
> (*Laughing.*)

...AND THEN I RAN ALL THE WAY HOME. I WAS SITTING AT THE TABLE FINISHING MY DINNER WHEN HE FINALLY CAME IN. I WAVED HIS BELT AT HIM AND SAID, "YOU'RE LATE!!"....OH, BOY...(*Laughing.*) HE CHASED ME ALL OVER THE HOUSE.....
(*Shaking his head.*)
DON'T MISUNDERSTAND ME. I LOVED MY HOME AND MY FAMILY, BUT I WOULD RATHER BE AT THE SCHOOL WITH MY PEERS WHO COULD UNDERSTAND ME PERFECTLY. I WAS KIND OF A TROUBLE-MAKER AT SCHOOL. I WAS BORED BECAUSE THEY PUT ME IN THE CLASSES WITH THE SLOWER-LEARNERS. AT THE TIME, TEACHERS USED ORAL METHODS AND SPEECHREADING. LATER, THEY USED SIGNED ENGLISH. THE MAJORITY OF STUDENTS BELIEVED THESE FORMS OF COMMUNICATION REFLECTED A SUPERIOR INTELLIGENCE WHILE THE USE OF ASL REFLECTED INFERIOR INTELLIGENCE. ASL WAS USED BY THE SLOW-LEARNERS. I HAPPENED TO USE ASL.

Spotlight comes up on MARK BULIGAN, *a young man with long hair and full beard. He wears "hippie" clothes.*

MARK BULIGAN
(*Using Signed English and voicing.*)

Gary has had no difficulty in mathematics during the past year. He has found math fairly easy and has mastered all the concepts. However, he still is not careful when reading verbal problems and often makes careless errors due to misunderstanding the problem. He has a tendency to fool around and distract others when he finishes his work.

Spotlight goes out on MARK BULIGAN *and up on* MARY LAMONT, *a middle-aged woman.*

MARY LAMONT
(*Signing fluently and voicing.*)

My most vivid recollections of Gary are centered on a science course that I taught. He was my most challenging student because he questioned everything. However, he was having difficulty getting good grades in the course. We had many closed-door, heart-to-heart talks in my classroom after class.

Spotlight out on MARY LAMONT *and back up on* GARY.

GARY

MARK BULIGAN TAUGHT MATH AND MARY LAMONT TAUGHT SCIENCE. THEY WOULD CLOSE THE CLASSROOM DOOR AND SIGN TO ME. SHE COULD HAVE GOTTEN IN TO A LOT OF TROUBLE FOR DEFYING THE SCHOOL'S COMMUNICATION

POLICY. WE HAD A GREAT TIME. I MEAN I WAS ABLE TO RESPOND AND WE REALLY UNDERSTOOD EACH OTHER. I WAS GOOD IN MATH AND SCIENCE. MR. BULIGAN AND MRS. LAMONT LOBBIED AND GOT ME MOVED OUT OF THE VOCATIONAL STUDENTS STREAM INTO THE ACADEMIC STREAM. AT FIRST, IT WAS NOT CLEAR THAT THE SCHOOL DID THE RIGHT THING MOVING ME UP.....

Lights up on a high school classroom. There are a couple of student chairs and a teacher's desk. YOUNG GARY sits in one of the chairs while MARK BULIGAN, sits on his desk looking at YOUNG GARY.

BULIGAN
(*Signing and voicing.*)

Do you want to be a good student?

YOUNG GARY

YES.

BULIGAN

Then you must improve your attitude towards your work.

YOUNG GARY

I'M TRYING....

BULIGAN

Come on, man....You're going to need to do much, much better if you want to go to Gallaudet.

19

YOUNG GARY
WHAT'S GALLAUDET?

BULIGAN
You don't know what Gallaudet is?

YOUNG GARY
NO. SHOULD I KNOW?

BULIGAN
Yes! Gallaudet is a university. G-A-L-L-A-U-D-E-T. Gallaudet University is the only university in the world for the deaf.

YOUNG GARY
REALLY? THERE'S A UNIVERSITY FOR ONLY DEAF PEOPLE?

BULIGAN
Yes! Do you want to go there?

YOUNG GARY
YES, MAYBE.

BULIGAN
Why 'maybe'?

YOUNG GARY
WHERE IS IT?

BULIGAN
Washington, D.C.

YOUNG GARY
AMERICA? WHERE THE PRESIDENT LIVES?

BULIGAN

Yes. But the Canadian government will give you money to go there, if you are a good student.

YOUNG GARY

REALLY?

BULIGAN

Yes!!! Tell me, what do you want to be when you grow up?

YOUNG GARY

I DON'T KNOW. I'M GOOD AT MATH. MAYBE I COULD BE A MATH TEACHER.

BULIGAN

Maybe you can. You can go to Gallaudet and get your degree in math and teaching. Maybe you can come back here and teach deaf students. But you must improve your attitude towards your school work. Man, you need this stuff. You need to be working a lot harder. You need to be hungry to learn as much as you can. And you need to dream bigger.

YOUNG GARY *nods his head in agreement as the lights cross-fade from the scene to a spotlight on* GARY.

GARY

OTHER TEACHERS AND GUIDANCE COUNSELORS WERE NOT SUPPORTIVE OF ME GOING TO GALLAUDET. THEY DIDN'T EVEN THINK I SHOULD BE ALLOWED TO TAKE THE EXTRANCE EXAM. IN MY FINAL YEAR OF HIGH SCHOOL, MY FELLOW

STUDENTS COMMONLY REFERRED TO ME AS AN ACADEMIC LOSER. I WAS TAUNTED BY THEM FOR TAKING THE GALLAUDET EXAM. THEY THOUGHT THIS WAS A BIG JOKE. HOWEVER, I DID TAKE IT AND EVERYONE WAS SURPRISED WHEN I PASSED, WHILE MANY OF THOSE WHO HAD TAUNTED ME FAILED.

MANY OF THE TEACHERS WERE IN COMPLETE SHOCK. THEY CALLED THE GUIDANCE COUNSELOR AND TOLD HIM TO CONVINCE ME THAT I SHOULDN'T GO TO GALLAUDET. THEY EVEN CALLED MY PARENTS. THEY FELT IT WAS GOING TO BE TOO DIFFICULT FOR ME. THEY SAID THAT MY ENGLISH WASN'T THAT GREAT. THEY WERE AFRAID IF I FAILED IT WOULD LOOK BAD ON THEM AND OUR SCHOOL.

BUT I WANTED TO GO TO GALLAUDET. THE ONLY REASON WAS BECAUSE MY FRIENDS WANTED TO GO THERE. I HAD NO CONCEPT OF WHAT I WANTED TO BECOME. I JUST MADE UP THE IDEA THAT I WANTED TO BE A MATH TEACHER, BECAUSE I FIGURED I WAS GOOD IN MATH. BUT REALLY, I DIDN'T WANT TO BE LEFT BEHIND.

Spotlight fades on GARY *and one comes up on* YOUNG GARY *and another on* NARRATOR. YOUNG GARY *opens an envelope. As he reads the letter, the* NARRATOR *signs.*

NARRATOR

DEAR MR. MALKOWSKI, I AM PLEASED TO ANNOUNCE THAT YOU HAVE BEEN ADMITTED TO GALLAUDET UNIVERSITY FOR THE 1976 FALL TERM. IN MAKING THIS DECISION, WE CONSIDERED THAT YOUR EXCELLENT POTENTIAL FOR COLLEGE WORK OUTWEIGHS YOUR DEFICIENCY IN KNOWLEDGE OF THE MEANING OF WORDS, IN THE AREA OF CORRECT GRAMMAR AND USAGE, AND IN THE ABILITY TO WRITE CLEAR AND CORRECT SENTENCES. THIS MEANS THAT WE BELIEVE YOU CAN HAVE A SUCCESSFUL COLLEGE CAREER IF YOU MAKE A DETERMINED EFFORT TO IMPROVE YOUR VOCABULARY, GRAMMAR AND WRITING ABILITY. WE RECOMMEND THAT YOU CONSIDER ATTENDING THE EIGHT-WEEK TUTORIAL SESSION THAT WILL BE OFFERED THIS SUMMER....WE LOOK FORWARD TO WELCOMING YOU ON CAMPUS....

YOUNG GARY *drops the letter, leaps into the air and hoots. Lights out. Spotlight up on* GARY.

GARY

WHEN I FIRST SET FOOT ON THE GALLAUDET CAMPUS I WAS SHOCKED. IT WAS CULTURE SHOCK OF THE MOST LITERAL KIND. THERE I WAS A CANADIAN KID WHO'D BEEN BROUGHT UP IN A SYSTEM THAT BASICALLY SAID I WAS TO HIDE MY DEAFNESS AND PRETEND I WAS A HEARING PERSON AS MUCH AS POSSIBLE. AND HERE WERE PEOPLE WHO WERE ALL

SPEAKING IN OUR OWN LANGUAGE AS THOUGH THEY WERE PROUD OF IT. PROUD TO BE DEAF. FOR THE FIRST TIME, I REALIZED THAT I HAD AN IDENTITY THAT WAS INDEED SOMETHING THAT WAS NOT FULLY SHARED BY MANY OTHER PEOPLE. I WAS PART OF A REAL COMMUNITY. A CULTURE THAT HEARING PEOPLE SIMPLY CANNOT BE A PART OF. AND THAT ENVIRONMENT, THAT DISCOVERY, IS SOMETHING EVERY DEAF PERSON DESERVES A CHANCE TO SHARE....

Lights up on a Gallaudet Dining Hall. Groups of young people are carrying on animated conversations all over the place. YOUNG GARY stands center stage, with a tray of food and tries to take it all in. He is simply in awe.

GARY

...IT WAS JUST OVERWHELMING! THE TEACHERS ALL COULD SIGN. SOME OF THE HEARING TEACHERS WERE USING ASL, SOME USED SIM-COM. SOME OF THEM WERE HEARING, BUT HAD PARENTS WHO WERE DEAF. THE RESIDENTIAL STAFF, SOME OF THEM WERE DEAF, SOME HEARING. THEY ALL COULD SIGN. AT THE ADMINISTRATIVE LEVEL, YOU SAW PEOPLE WHO COULD SIGN. SOCIAL WORKERS, DOCTORS, LAWYERS, ENGINEERS. DISCUSSIONS, STUDENT ACTIVITIES AND DEBATES, WERE ALL IN SIGN. ASL WAS USED BY THE MAJORITY OF PEOPLE THERE. SIGNED ENGLISH AND SPEAKING, THEY WERE SUDDENLY IN THE

MINORITY. IT WAS SUDDENLY REVERSED.
I QUICKLY REALIZED THAT MY
LANGUAGE, ASL, WAS IMPORTANT.

YOUNG GARY *sits down at a table alone.   Lights out on GARY and a spotlight up on* JAMES TUCKER. *He is a student at Gallaudet.*

JAMES TUCKER
(*Voicing and signing.*)

If I had to pick a student who benefited the most from the Gallaudet experience, it would be Gary. He blossomed so much there. I remember thinking when I first met him, 'He won't last a semester here.'
(*Picks up a tray and goes to* YOUNG GARY.)
CAN I SIT HERE?
(*YOUNG GARY nods as he chews a mouthful of food.*)
WHY ARE YOU SITTING ALONE?
(*YOUNG GARY shrugs and continues to chew his food and shove in more. JAMES starts to eat too.*)
YOU'RE FROM CANADA RIGHT?
(*YOUNG GARY nods.*)
HOW DO YOU LIKE GALLAUDET?

YOUNG GARY

IT'S HARDER THAN I EXPECTED.   THE
EXPECTATIONS ARE HIGH HERE.

JAMES
WHAT DO YOU MEAN?

YOUNG GARY

STUDENTS HERE ARE EXPECTED TO WRITE ESSAYS AND DO RESEARCH. THAT KIND OF THING WAS NEVER EXPECTED OF ME AT MILTON.

JAMES

REALLY?

YOUNG GARY

YES, I AM SERIOUS. THIS IS A LEARNING EXPERIENCE.

JAMES
(*Laughing.*)

YES. THIS IS A UNIVERSITY. THAT'S WHAT YOU'RE SUPPOSED TO DO, LEARN!

YOUNG GARY
(*Laughing.*)

YEAH, I KNOW. I NEED TO CATCH UP WITH THE OTHER STUDENTS LIKE YOU. WILL YOU HELP ME? YOU KNOW, I NEED TO IMPROVE MY ENGLISH. I TURNED IN A PAPER AND THE TEACHER ASKED, 'DID YOU WRITE THIS?' AND WHEN I SAID I DID, SHE SAID, 'OH, MY GOODNESS! YOU'RE NOT REALLY COLLEGE MATERIAL. YOU BETTER GET MORE HELP IN ENGLISH OR YOU ARE NOT GOING TO STAY AT GALLAUDET.' IT WOULD BREAK MY HEART IF I HAD TO LEAVE HERE. CAN YOU HELP?

JAMES

YOU NEED TO GO TO THE ENGLISH TUTORIAL CENTER AND GET A TUTOR.

YOUNG GARY

I KNOW. I DID THAT. I JUST WANT AS MUCH HELP AS I CAN GET. YOU'RE SMART. I WANT TO BE ABLE TO ASK YOU FOR HELP. CAN I?

JAMES

SURE. NO PROBLEM.

YOUNG GARY

OK. THANKS. OK, I HAVE A QUESTION FOR YOU NOW. WHAT DOES 'A-C-C-O-M-P-L-I-S-H-M-E-N-T' MEAN?

JAMES

ACCOMPLISHMENT?

YOUNG GARY

YEAH, I THINK SO. TODAY, I WAS IN WORLD CIVILIZATION CLASS AND DR. SMITS SAID SOMETHING ABOUT 'ACCOMPLISHMENT' AND I INTERRUPTED AND ASKED WHAT DOES IT MEAN.

JAMES

WHAT DID SMITS SAY?

YOUNG GARY

'WHAT ARE YOU DOING AT GALLAUDET IF YOU DON'T UNDERSTAND WORDS LIKE THESE?'

(Rolling his eyes.)
I WAS VERY EMBARRASSED.

JAMES
(Laughing.)
YEAH, I'M SURE.

YOUNG GARY
SO WHAT DOES 'ACCOMPLISHMENT' MEAN?!

JAMES
IT MEANS WHEN YOU HAVE REACHED A GOAL. THEN YOU HAVE AN ACCOMPLISHMENT. THE THING YOU DID TO REACH A GOAL IS AN ACCOMPLISHMENT. GET IT?

YOUNG GARY
NOT REALLY.

JAMES
IT'S LIKE YOU PASSING THE ENTRANCE EXAM AND GETTING INTO GALLAUDET. THAT WAS AN ACCOMPLISHMENT. SO ANYTHING YOU ACHIEVE IS AN ACCOMPLISHMENT.

YOUNG GARY
'ACHIEVE'?! WHAT'S THAT MEAN?

JAMES
ACCOMPLISH. IT MEANS THE SAME THING. ACHIEVEMENT. ACCOMPLISHMENT.

ACHIEVE. ACCOMPLISH. THEY MEAN THE SAME THING.

YOUNG GARY

I HATE ENGLISH. THERE'S SO MANY WORDS AND SO MANY MEAN THE SAME THING!
(Sighing.)
THERE'S SO MUCH TO LEARN.

JAMES

THAT'S WHY YOU'RE HERE.

YOUNG GARY

I KNOW. AND I WANT TO STAY HERE! THANKS FOR HELPING. I'LL SEE YOU LATER.

JAMES

WHERE ARE YOU GOING?

YOUNG GARY

THE PUB!

Lights out on the scene and a spotlight comes up on LINDA.

LINDA
(Signing as she speaks.)

When he first got to Gallaudet, Gary had the best time. Especially the first year. He hardly had any money for food because any money he got he'd spend on beer, which is really ironic, because he doesn't even drink. He'd buy all this beer and stuff for people at Gallaudet to try and make friends.

29

And he did! So for him to make connections and interact was very important.

Spotlight up on GARY.

GARY

I SPENT MY MONEY AT THE PUB BECAUSE OF PEER PRESSURE. I USED BEER AS A PROP TO BRAG THAT I AM ONE OF THE GROUP WHO COULD DRINK. BUT ONE TIME I GOT DRUNK AND I FELL ASLEEP IN A BUSH. THE CAMPUS POLICE WOKE ME UP THE NEXT MORNING. I DIDN'T LIKE THAT EXPERIENCE. IT WAS NOT A GREAT ACCOMPLISHMENT. I DIDN'T EVER DRINK AGAIN AFTER THAT. I STILL DON'T LIKE THE TASTE OF ALCOHOL. IT WAS A GOOD THING FOR ME TO GO THROUGH.

LINDA

That first year a bunch of male students shaved their heads and Gary participated. He'd do almost anything to fit in. He shaved all his hair off! It was the clown in him coming out. Vying for attention. He didn't take things too seriously then.

Lights out on LINDA *crossfade up to* JAMES.

JAMES
(Voicing and signing.)

Gary stood out in the Gallaudet crowd because of a lot of things. One big thing was he was poor and wore ill-fitting clothes. He told me they were hand-me-downs from his brother. The sign name the Gallaudet community gave him was 'Canadian Polack.' We students teased him and called him a

Polack because of his last name and his occasional
clumsiness or stupidity. I can't remember any
specific incident. Maybe it was just his appearance.
He used to wear these extremely short Addias
shorts. They were European. The really ugly kind,
right-up-your-crack type.

GARY
(*Laughing at* JAMES.)

JAMIE TUCKER WAS PART OF THE
GALLAUDET ELITE. HIS ASL WAS
BEAUTIFUL. HIS PARENTS WERE DEAF. HE
WAS VERY CONFIDENT, OFTEN FULL OF
HIMSELF, EVEN, ARROGANT AT TIMES.
WHEN I TRIED TO JOIN TUCKER'S ELITE
CLIQUE OF DEAF FROM DEAF, THE GROUP
WOULD JUST LOOK AT ME AND ACT LIKE
'WHO'S THAT GUY?!'
(JAMES *laughs as spot fades on him.*)
I ACTUALLY TRIED TO MIX WITH EVERY
GROUP AT GALLAUDET. IT WAS A
LEARNING EXPERIENCE AND I WANTED IT
ALL. I WANTED TO BE INVOLVED IN
EVERYTHING. ONE TIME I WENT TO A
CHRISTIAN GROUP EVENT AND ANOTHER
TIME I WENT TO A GAY AND LESBIAN
GROUP MEETING. I JUST WANTED TO GO
AND SEE WHAT THEY WERE ALL ABOUT. I
WAS A FREE SPIRIT THEN. THE CANADIAN
CLUB CALLED ME 'THE LOST SHEEP OF
CANADA.' I GUESS PEOPLE BACK THEN
THOUGHT I WAS A BIT OF A GOOF.

JAMES
(*Signing and speaking.*)

Gary became very popular at Gallaudet. When I recall him there, I don't remember anyone ever getting mad at him. He was really well liked by everyone. Yes, he was a little strange because of his European clothing or his early baldness, but he was well liked. I. King Jordan who had Gary as a student in one of his classes long before he became president of Gallaudet, says Gary can carry on a conversation with a fire hydrant! Gary likes to draw people out and learn what they are thinking. This is a good skill for a politician, don't you agree?

GARY

I BECAME INVOLVED IN STUDENT POLITICS IN 1980. I HAD A CABINET POSITION IN THE STUDENT GOVERNMENT AND I WAS PRESIDENT OF THE CANADIAN CLUB. I BEGAN TO MEET POLITICALLY ACTIVE PEOPLE LIKE PATTY SHORES WHO WAS FROM CANADA TOO, AND WOULD BECOME THE STUDENT BODY GOVERNMENT PRESIDENT.

Spotlight up on PATTY SHORES.

PATTY SHORES

WHEN I MET GARY HE WAS PRESIDENT OF THE CANADIAN CLUB AND USED AN AUTHORITIAN APPROACH. I CHALLENGED HIM AND DEMANDED THE DEMOCRATIC APPROACH. AT THAT TIME GARY WAS INTELLECTUALLY CURIOUS BUT SOCIALLY IMMATURE AND HYPERACTIVE. HE WAS

ALWAYS FIGHTING AGAINST PREJUDICE, DISCRIMINATION AND ALWAYS ASKING FOR EVIDENCE, EXPLANATIONS AND CLARITY.

JAMES

Gary did drive people crazy sometimes because he was a borderline pest, but as he grew older, like the rest of us, he made more sense, was able to formulate his own ideas, and become more articulate in expressing them. Gary became more and more polished and in his senior year he had the self-confidence. Gallaudet is famous for its bull sessions. Gary would jump in and capture the floor...

The spotlights on GARY, JAMES and PATTY fade out.

Lights up full on a Gallaudet University cafeteria. GARY, JAMES and PATTY join the scene which has a group of students in a half circle sitting on chairs and tables, taking turns speaking in a very animated discussion.

GARY has removed his coat and tie and sits to the side, observing the debate. When GARY, JAMES and PATTY join the scene, GARY begins speaking.

GARY

...IN THE EYES OF THE CATHOLIC CHURCH AND IN THE HEARTS OF MANY PEOPLE ABORTION IS WRONG, BUT A WOMAN MUST HAVE THE RIGHT TO CONTROL HER OWN BODY. IT'S HER CHOICE. NO ONE HAS THE RIGHT TO TAKE THAT DECISION FROM HER. SO EVEN...

SO EVEN THOUGH I THINK ABORTION'S WRONG, IT IS NOT MY RIGHT TO SAY ANYONE MUST HAVE A CHILD THEY DON'T WANT TO HAVE. THOSE WHO OPPOSE ABORTION NEED TO EDUCATE YOUNG PEOPLE AND HELP PREVENT UNWANTED PREGNANCIES. AND WE SHOULDN'T PATRONIZE WOMEN AND TELL THEM WHAT THEY MUST DO, ANYMORE THAN HEARING PEOPLE WHO PATRONIZE US.

JAMES
(*Standing up and applauding.*)
WELL SAID....GOOD JOB, GARY.

Others join in, applauding with raised hands.

GARY
ARE YOU SURPRISED BY HOW MUCH I KNOW?

JAMES
YEAH, I AM.

PATTY
NOT BAD FOR A CANADIAN....

GARY
THANK YOU FOR YOUR SUPPORT.

PATTY
DO YOU KNOW SOMEBODY IS FALLING IN LOVE WITH YOU?

GARY

WHAT?!

PATTY

DO YOU KNOW SOMEBODY LOVES YOU?

GARY

YOU LOVE ME?

PATTY
(*Whacking him.*)
NO! YOU GOOF, NOT ME! HER!
(*She points at* MARY *who is chatting with someone and periodically glancing over at* GARY *and* PATTY.)

GARY
(*Checking her out.*)
HMMM.....SHE'S CUTE.

PATTY

SHE WAS GOOGLILY-EYED THE WHOLE TIME YOU WERE SPEAKING.

GARY

REALLY?

PATTY

YES! SHE'S HEAD OVER HEELS!

GARY

STOP!
(*Taking a peek at her.*)
WHAT'S HER NAME?

PATTY

M-A-R-Y C-I-M-I-C-A-T-A   SHE'S VERY
POPULAR. YOU HAVE SEEN HER BEFORE,
RIGHT?

GARY

YEAH, I THINK I HAD HER IN ONE OF MY
PSYCHOLOGY CLASSES.

PATTY

WELL, GO TALK TO HER.

GARY

NO. SHE'S TALKING TO SOMEONE NOW.

PATTY

GOOFY, SHE'S WAITING FOR YOU TO TALK
TO HER. NOW, GO OVER THERE OR I'M
GOING TO TELL EVERYONE IN THE
CANADIAN CLUB THAT YOU ARE NOT THE
LOST SHEEP, YOU ARE THE LOST CHICKEN.

PATTY *gives* GARY *a push in* MARY's *direction.*

GARY

HI, I'M G-A-R-Y M-A-L-O-W-S-K-I.   MY
FRIEND THERE SAID YOU WANTED TO
TALK TO ME.

MARY
(*Shakes her head.*)

NO.

GARY

REALLY?

MARY

I DON'T HAVE ANYTHING TO SAY.

GARY

OKAY.
                    (Starts to walk away. Stops.)
YOUR NAME IS MARY, RIGHT?

MARY

YES.

GARY

DIDN'T WE HAVE A CLASS TOGETHER?

MARY

YES.   PSYCHOLOGY 101.

GARY

OH,   YEAH.   RIGHT.   ARE   YOU   A
PSYCHOLOGY MAJOR?

MARY

NO, I AM SOCIAL WORK MAJOR.   SAME AS
YOU.

GARY

HOW DID YOU KNOW MY MAJOR?

MARY

PATTY TOLD ME.

GARY

WHAT ELSE DID PATTY TELL YOU?

MARY

YOU ARE FROM CANADA.

GARY

EVERYBODY KNOWS THAT. THEY CALL ME THE CANADIAN POLACK. SO WHERE ARE YOU FROM?

MARY

NEW JERSEY. I WENT TO M.K.S.D.

GARY

OH, I SEE. I KNOW SOME PEOPLE WHO WENT TO M.K.S.D. IS YOUR FAMILY HEARING OR DEAF?

MARY

HEARING. I HAVE 3 BROTHERS AND 2 SISTERS.

GARY

MY FAMILY IS ALL HEARING TOO. I HAVE 2 BROTHERS AND 2 SISTERS. I WENT TO SCHOOL IN MILTON, ONTARIO.

MARY

OH, I KNOW SOME PEOPLE WHO WENT THERE.

GARY

DO THEY KNOW ME?

MARY

YES.

GARY

EVERYBODY KNOWS ME.

MARY

I DON'T KNOW YOU.

GARY

DO YOU WANT TO KNOW ME?

MARY

MAYBE. (*Smiling.*) MAYBE NOT.

GARY
(*Laughing.*)

AH, GIVE ME A CHANCE. I AM NOT VERY
GOOD AT THIS. YOU HAVE TO HELP ME.

MARY

OKAY, ASK ME FOR A DATE.

GARY

WILL YOU SAY YES?

MARY

MAYBE. (*Laughing.*) MAYBE NOT.

GARY
(*Laughing with her.*)

YOU ARE VERY MEAN!

MARY

NO I AM NOT. ASK ME.

GARY

OK, BUT I WILL ONLY ASK ONE TIME. IF YOU SAY NO, I WILL NEVER ASK YOU AGAIN. THAT'S A WARNING.

MARY

IF I SAY NO NOW, I MIGHT SAY YES THE NEXT TIME.

GARY

REALLY?

MARY

ASK ME.

GARY

DO YOU WANT TO GO ON A DATE WITH ME?

MARY

MAYBE.

GARY
(*Laughing.*)
DO YOU WANT TO GO HAVE A DRINK?

MARY

I DON'T DRINK.

GARY

SAME WITH ME. I USED TO DRINK, BUT COULDN'T HANDLE IT. ONE NIGHT I WAS COMING HOME FROM THE PUB AND I FELL ASLEEP IN A BUSH.

MARY
(*Laughing.*)

REALLY?

GARY
YES. I KNOW I AM A GOOF.

MARY
NO YOU ARE NOT.

GARY
DO YOU WANT TO GO FOR A WALK?

MARY
WHERE?

GARY
TO YOUR DORM.

MARY
OKAY.

GARY
I'LL SHOW YOU THE BUSH I FEEL ASLEEP IN.

MARY *laughs. They start to exit together*.

GARY
SO ARE YOU GOING ON A DATE WITH ME?

MARY
(*Smiling.*)

MAYBE.

GARY *stops and steps into a spotlight, as* MARY *exits the stage.*

GARY
(*Speaking to the audience.*)

"MAYBE" BECAME "YES". MARY AND I BECAME CLOSE VERY QUICKLY. AND WE BECAME ENGAGED IN A FEW MONTHS BECAUSE MARY WAS PREGNANT. I WAS EMBARRASSED. I DON'T KNOW WHY WE DIDN'T USE BIRTH CONTROL. WE WERE YOUNG AND NOT MATURE BUT THERE WAS NEVER ANY QUESTION ABOUT WHAT WE WERE GOING TO DO. WE BOTH CAME FROM CATHOLIC FAMILIES....

I WAS ACTUALLY PLANNING TO GO WITH THE CATHOLIC CHURCH TO BANGLORE, INDIA TO WORK WITH THE POOR DEAF PEOPLE THERE.

I WAS HOPING TO MEET MOTHER THERESA. WHEN I HAD TO TELL MY PRIEST THAT I COULDN'T GO TO INDIA BECAUSE I WAS GETTING MARRIED, HE WAS SHOCKED. HE COULDN'T BELIEVE I WAS GETTING MARRIED. IT WAS MY DREAM TO GO TO INDIA...

MARY
(*Now in her own spotlight.*)

WHEN MY PARENTS CAME TO VISIT, THEY HAD A FIT WHEN THEY FOUND OUT I WAS PREGNANT. BUT WE GOT MARRIED ON MARCH 11, 1982. WE HAD TWO WEDDING RECEPTIONS. ONE WAS AT GALLAUDET. 150 PEOPLE CAME. THE SECOND WAS IN NEW JERSEY FOR MY FAMILY. GARY'S

PARENTS AND SISTER CAME FROM
CANADA FOR IT.

GARY

DURING THE FIRST COUPLE OF MONTHS OF
OUR MARRIAGE, WE CONTINUED TO LIVE
IN SEPARATE DORM ROOMS.   DURING
SUMMER SCHOOL, GALLAUDET LET US
LIVE TOGETHER IN THE DORMS. WE WERE
THE FIRST MARRIED COUPLE ALLOWED TO
LIVE TOGETHER IN THE DORMS. SO I GOT
MY B.A. DEGREE IN SOCIAL WORK AND
PSYCHOLOGY IN MAY AND I DECIDED TO
GO TO GRADUATE SCHOOL BECAUSE OF
PEER PRESSURE. MANY FRIENDS OF MINE
WERE PLANNING TO STUDY FOR A
MASTER'S DEGREE AND THERE WERE
FUNDS AVAILABLE TO SUPPORT MY
STUDIES.   I APPLIED TO GALLAUDET'S
REHABILIATION COUNSELING PROGRAM
AND I WAS ACCEPTED, BUT ON A
CONDITIONAL BASIS BECAUSE I HAD A "C"
AVERAGE IN MY UNDERGRAD COURSES.
THEY DECIDED TO GIVE ME A CHANCE TO
SEE HOW THINGS WOULD GO FOR A
SEMESTER.

MARY

BEFORE GARY STARTED GRAD SCHOOL IN
THE FALL WE MOVED INTO OUR OWN
APARTMENT OFF CAMPUS AND OUR
DAUGHTER WAS BORN ON HIS FIRST DAY
OF GRADUATE SCHOOL, AUGUST 20.

GARY

AFTER THE BABY WAS BORN, I CALLED MY
PARENTS AND MY IN-LAWS AND TOLD
THEM OUR BABY GIRL, CARLEE, HAD
ARRIVED SAFELY.   THEN I DROVE MY
BROWN   '73   MALIBU   CHEVY   ON
MACARTHUR BOULEVARD, PAST ALL THE
EMBASSIES AND ALL OVER WASHINGTON,
DC HONKING THE HORN UNTIL I GOT TO
GALLAUDET.   I BOUGHT CHOCOLATE
CIGARS AND HANDED THEM OUT TO MY
COLLEGE FRIENDS AND CLASSMATES.

GARY *and* MARY *leave the spotlights and walk into a
small apartment setting, perhaps just a couch and a coffee
table.* MARY *picks up a bundle and cradles it as they move
into the scene.*

GARY

WELCOME HOME MOTHER AND BABY.

MARY

AH, LOOK AT ALL THE FLOWERS.

GARY

WE RECEIVED LOTS OF GIFTS TOO FOR
CARLEE.

MARY
(*Sitting down with the baby.*)
NICE TO BE HOME.

GARY
IS SHE STILL SLEEPING?

MARY

YES. SHE IS BEAUTIFUL.

GARY

YES. SHE SLEEPS A LOT.

MARY

YES, THAT'S WHAT BABIES DO WHEN THEY
ARE NEW.

GARY

I HOPE SHE'S DEAF. (*Pause.*) DO YOU HOPE
SHE'S DEAF?

MARY

I DON'T CARE AS LONG AS SHE IS A
HEALTHY BABY.

GARY

SHOULD WE TEST HER?

MARY

WHY?

GARY

TO SEE IF SHE'S DEAF.

MARY

I DON'T KNOW. SHE IS SLEEPING.....

GARY

BEST TIME TO TEST HER. I WILL BANG
SOME POTS AND IF SHE WAKES UP, WE'LL
KNOW.

                    MARY
    OKAY. FINE.

GARY *runs off and then back on with a pot and a silver spoon. He begins whacking on the metal pot with the spoon, making a big racket as he marches around the room. The baby stirs in* MARY *arms and begins crying. GARY and* MARY *exchange looks. He drops the pot and spoon.*

                    GARY
    I CAN'T BELIEVE IT! SHE'S HEARING.

                    MARY
                    (*Rocking the baby back to sleep.*)
    YES.

                    GARY
    ARE YOU SAD?

                    MARY
    NO. I TOLD YOU I DIDN'T CARE. ARE YOU
    SAD?

                    GARY
    NO....BUT I AM DISAPPOINTED.

                    MARY
    WHY?

                    GARY
    I WANTED HER TO BE LIKE US.

                    MARY
    WE CAN TEACH HER SIGN LANGUAGE. SHE
    WILL BE ABLE TO COMMUNICATE WITH US.

GARY

YEAH, I KNOW

MARY

(*Laughing.*)

BE HAPPY. SHE IS HEALTHY. THAT'S ALL THAT'S IMPORTANT.

GARY

(*Stepping out of the scene and speaking to the audience.*)

WHEN I DISCOVERED CARLEE WAS HEARING IT FORCED ME TO CONFRONT MY HATRED FOR HEARING PEOPLE. I HATED HEARING PEOPLE BECAUSE OF THE WAY THEY HAD OPPRESSED DEAF PEOPLE. THEN I REALIZED IF I CONTINUED TO HATE HEARING PEOPLE THEN I COULDN'T LOVE MY DAUGHTER. WHEN CARLEE WAS BORN I LEARNED ABOUT THE RESPONSIBILITIES OF BEING A FATHER. IT WAS AN EXCITING EXPERIENCE TO SEE MY BEAUTIFUL DAUGHTER AND HAVE A HAPPY FAMILY EVEN THOUGH I WAS UNDER PRESSURE DUE TO GRAD SCHOOL. I ENJOYED BEING A HUSBAND AND A FATHER.

MARY

DURING GRADUATE SCHOOL, GARY WORKED THREE JOBS SO I COULD FINISH GALLAUDET AND GET MY DEGREE. I WANTED TO DROP OUT, BUT HE WOULDN'T LET ME. WE GOT ALONG WELL AND IF WE HAD ARGUMENTS IT WAS MOSTLY ABOUT WHOSE TURN IT WAS TO LOOK AFTER CARLEE SO THE OTHER COULD STUDY.

Spotlight out on MARY.

GARY

I LIKED GRADUATE SCHOOL, BUT I BEGAN TO GET VERY FRUSTRATED WITH THE COMMUNICATION METHODS. I WAS MISSING A LOT IN THE LECTURES. MOST OF THE PROFESSORS USED SIM-COM IN THE CLASSROOM AND I DID NOT COMPLETELY UNDERSTAND WHAT THEY WERE SAYING. AND MANY HEARING GRADUATE STUDENTS USED THEIR MINIMAL SIGN LANGUAGE SKILLS IN CLASSROOM DISCUSSIONS. SO I REQUESTED AN ASL INTERPRETER.

Spotlight up on JAMES TUCKER.

JAMES
(*Innocently.*)
DID YOU EXPERIENCE ANY RESISTENCE?

GARY
(*Laughing.*)
OH, YES. GALLAUDET HAD A TRADITION THAT MANY HEAING PROFESSORS AND HEARING GRADUATE STUDENTS AND EVEN SOME DEAF STUDENTS USED SIM-COM, THAT'S VOICING AND SIGNING IN ENGLISH, INSTEAD OF ASL, IN THE CLASSROOM. NO ONE CHALLENGED THIS TRADITION. IT WAS BIG NEWS ON CAMPUS AND I WAS CRITICIZED BY SEVERAL DEAF FACULTY AND STAFF MEMBERS, THOUGH I DID GET PRAISE FROM OTHERS, FOR CHALLENGING

GALLAUDET TO PROVIDE ME WITH AN ASL INTERPRETER AND NOT ACCEPTING INCOMPLETE COMMUNICATION.

JAMES

GARY'S REQUEST FOR AN ASL INTERPRETER WAS A RADICAL IDEA BACK THEN. THE DEAF COMMUNITY BY AND LARGE WAS UNSCHOOLED IN ASL LINGUISTICS AND ACCEPTED SIM-COM AS THE 'HIGH' LANGUAGE FOR ACADEMICS. TODAY, ASL INTERPRETERS IN CLASSROOMS ARE PART OF THE GALLAUDET UNIVERSITY LANDSCAPE. GARY WAS GAINING A WELL-EARNED REPUTATION AS A SHIT-DISTURBER AND IT CONTINUED ON THROUGH GRADUATE SCHOOL. EVERYWHERE HE WENT HE BEGAN TO DEMAND BETTER ACCESS AND SERVICES.

Spotlight out on JAMES.

GARY

I BEGAN TO STEP ON A LOT OF TOES. I ALMOST DIDN'T GET MY MASTER'S DEGREE. I HAD BEEN WORKING FOR DIFFERENT AGENCIES THAT SERVICE THE DEAF, I WAS WORKING AS A COUNSELOR AND MY COUNSELING PHILOSOPHY OF 'EMPOWERMENT' AT THE TIME WAS DIFFERENT THAN THE AGENCY'S. ONE OF MY CO-WORKERS INFORMED ON ME AND I WAS ALSO ACCUSED OF RELEASING CONFIDENTIAL INFORMATION AT PUBLIC MEETINGS. FORTUNATELY, I WAS ABLE TO

Richard Medugno

DEFEND MYSELF AND I HAD SEVERAL
LETTERS OF RECOMMENDATION FROM MY
SUPERVISORS. SO I GOT MY MASTER'S
DEGREE IN REHABILITATION COUNSELING
IN 1984 AND MARY COMPLETED HER B.A. IN
SOCIAL WORK. I HAD BEEN AT
GALLAUDET FOR EIGHT YEARS AND I WAS
READY TO GO BACK TO CANADA. I
STARTED CONTACTING MY OLD FRIENDS
AT MILTON ABOUT FINDING WORK.

MARY LAMONT
(*Signing fluently and voicing.*)

Dear Gary, I was really thrilled to get your note
with your resume and inquiry about future
employment here. I've taken the liberty of
circulating your resume to the superintendent and
program directors of both the school and residences.
In this way they will be aware of someone of your
skills, who is interested in upcoming positions. I
am not aware of anything at the present time. It is
so nice for an 'old' teacher like me to hear about
my successful former students. I can remember you
in my classes very well and I remember feeling that
if I could only convince this kid that he has
potential, he would do so well. Well, I'm not sure
how much influence I had, but I am really proud of
what you've done and are doing to help others. I
hope by spreading your resume around that
something good will happen and we'll have you
back in Canada where we need deaf leaders badly.
Yours truly, Mary Lamont.

Spotlight crossfades from MARY LAMONT *to* IRIS
BOSHES.

IRIS
(*Signing and voicing.*)

I'm Iris Boshes.   Gary applied for a position at the Canadian Hearing Society for a vocational rehab counselor.   One of my responsibilities as Director of Rehabilitation was to oversee the counseling programs.   I remember discussing hiring Gary with the executive director, Denis Morrice....

Lights up on an office setting.   One side of the desk sits IRIS.   *Enters* DENIS MORRICE *with a piece of paper in hand.*

DENIS

I checked his references.   They say he's good but—
(*He hands her the paper.*)
He's a shit-disturber.

IRIS

Hmmmm...I'm not so sure if that's the kind of person we want to hire.

DENIS

Yeah, but maybe it's time we got someone in here to stir things up a bit.

IRIS

Yes, I know what you mean....Tell me this, what if we guide him to advocating and get things happening without being negative?   Do you think we could succeed?

DENIS

Possibly, but he could be tough to handle.

                    IRIS
Are you up to it?

                    DENIS
I don't know.

                    IRIS
We need someone with creative ideas.

                    DENIS
Yeah.   Let's hire him.   He is so persistent.   He's
constantly calling me on the TTY and sending his
resume.   I must have 12 copies.

                    IRIS
Okay, let's hire him.

                    GARY
                 (*In the spotlight.*)
WHEN I BEGAN WORKING AT THE
CANADIAN HEARING SOCIETY IN TORONTO
IN MARCH, 1985, I WAS ONE OF A HANDFUL
OF DEAF COUNSELORS EMPLOYED THERE.
DENIS   MORRICE,   THE   EXECUTIVE
DIRECTOR OF CHS AT THE TIME, BELIEVED
IN EMPOWERMENT AND BROUGHT A LOT
OF   DEAF   PEOPLE   INTO   THE
ORGANIZATION.

                    DENIS
                (*Signing and voicing.*)
Gary's influence on CHS was to help everyone's
attitude and keep everyone focused.

GARY
(*Joining the office setting.*)

LET'S REMEMBER WHY WE'RE HERE. WE'RE HERE FOR DEAF PEOPLE. THIS ISN'T SOME LITTLE SOCIAL SERVICE ORGANIZATION. IT'S ABOUT DEAF PEOPLE'S RIGHTS.

DENIS

He kept us on our toes all the time. He challenged. I always appreciated meeting with him because he helped me stay focused. He helped me to know what should happen next. I don't pretend to understand deafness. I accept it. It's a culture. You just have to appreciate the culture. It's the only disability that has it's own culture. I never felt I could truly understand deafness, but there was no reason I couldn't accept it. And Gary helped me work through that and what should be done and what direction we should take things.

KAREN *moves on to the office setting joining* IRIS *and* DENIS.

KAREN
(*Signing and voicing.*)

When Gary started at CHS, he frightened people, I think. He wouldn't tolerate the bad signing going on in staff meetings and demanded an ASL interpreter be provided. I didn't like Gary at first. He was rude and abrupt. He never let an opportunity to criticize the hearing staff go by. Gary doesn't have any problems working in a place where there's a lot of hostility. (She laughs.)

DENIS

I think Gary probably upset some people. If, as Karen has said, he would challenge hearing people every single time, that would wear on a person, especially if it's a counselor working her butt off and then makes a small faux-pas and they have this guy jumping down her throat. I never saw him as a trouble-maker. In fact, I counted on him a lot to stir up things. I saw this as a way of getting the organization to grow.

IRIS
(Signing and voicing.)

What impressed me about Gary was that he was straightforward all the time. He was always outspoken. If he saw screw-ups, he would point it out. He was always questioning. At the time of his hiring, there were only a few other deaf people on staff. It was good having Gary on staff because it gave CHS credibility with the Deaf community. Gary was a good link. The Deaf community was not easy to work with. Gary was very politically astute, knowing how to approach people and influence them.

KAREN
(Signing and voicing.)

VR counselors are responsible for helping students find training and schooling. They work with people around their vocational goals. Not finding the jobs, but finding the skills necessary and reaching potential. Gary's approach to counseling was to empower people. He worked with his clients to give them confidence in their abilities and help them understand what deaf people could do. You know he served as a role model for them.

GARY

IT IS IMPORTANT TO ME AS A V.R.
COUNSELOR TO LOOK AT MY CLIENTS IN
TERMS OF THEIR APTITUDES AND THEIR
SKILLS AND TO ENCOURAGE THE
DEVELOPMENT OF THEIR POTENTIAL IN
RELATIONSHIP TO THEIR WORK SKILLS.
AND I NEVER DISCOURAGE A CLIENT FROM
A JOB, I WOULD HELP THEM DISCOVER
WHETHER THEY HAVE THE ABILITY AND
APTITUDE.

A young female STUDENT *comes into the scene and sits
down, while his co-workers take a few steps back,* GARY
greets the student.

GARY

SO YOU WOULD LIKE TO BE A
RECEPTIONIST?

STUDENT

YES. I THINK IT WOULD BE FUN TO GREET
PEOPLE.

GARY
(*Nodding.*)

A RECPTIONIST IS AN IMPORTANT
POSITION. EVERY COMPANY NEEDS ONE
TO WELCOME VISITORS. YOU KNOW A
RECEPTIONIST ALSO ANSWERS PHONE
CALLS RIGHT?

STUDENT

YES.

GARY

HOW MUCH HEARING DO YOU HAVE? ARE YOU ABLE TO FUNCTION ON THE TELEPHONE?

STUDENT

I HAVE SOME HEARING, BUT I HAVE TO USE A TTY.

GARY

AND YOUR SPEECH?

STUDENT

MOST PEOPLE CAN UNDERSTAND ME.

GARY

YOU ARE A FRIENDLY PERSON AND VERY BRIGHT. THERE ARE A LOT OF POSITIONS THAT YOU COULD WORK WELL IN. BEING A RECEPTIONIST IS A GOOD THING, BUT I THINK YOU WILL WANT TO DO MORE AFTER SOME TIME. YOU HAVE A LOT OF POTENTIAL AND YOU NEED TO WORK ON DEVELOPING IT TAKING CLASSES OR GOING TO COLLEGE. WHY NOT AIM HIGHER? WHY NOT HAVE BIGGER DREAMS?

STUDENT

LIKE WHAT?

GARY

WELL, WHAT DO YOU LIKE TO DO? WHAT WORK EXPERIENCE HAVE YOU HAD THAT YOU ENJOY AND ARE GOOD AT?

STUDENT

I LIKE HELPING PEOPLE. I WORKED IN MY
DAD'S STORE MAKING FLOWER
ARRANGEMENTS.

GARY

DID YOU LIKE THAT?

STUDENT

YES.

GARY

WELL, YOU GOT GOOD EXPERIENCE
LEARNING ABOUT HOW A SMALL
BUSINESS WORKS. MAYBE YOU COULD
TAKE BUSINESS CLASSES AND START
YOUR OWN BUSINESS.

STUDENT

DO YOU REALLY THINK I COULD DO THAT?

GARY

YES, OF COURSE. YOU CAN DO ANYTHING
YOU WANT TO DO. WHY LIMIT YOURSELF?
> (Steps out of the scene and speaks
> directly to the audience.)

MY JOB AS A V.R. COUNSELOR IS TO ASSIST
MY CLIENTS TO BECOME EMPLOYED AND
FULLY INDEPENDENT. MY SECOND GOAL
IS TO ENCOURAGE A FEELING OF PRIDE IN
THEMSELVES AND IN DEAF CULTURE. I
FEEL BOTH OF THESE THINGS HELP MY
DEAF CLIENTS FUNCTION MORE
POSITIVELY AND COMPETITIVELY IN THE
HEARING WORLD. I FEEL THAT IT IS

IMPORTANT THAT DEAF PEOPLE LEARN ABOUT THE HEARING AND THE DEAF WORLDS. THIS MAY HELP THEM COPE WITH THE DIFFICULTIES OF EVERYDAY LIFE.

IRIS
(*Signing and voicing.*)

During his time at the Canadian Hearing Society, Gary was involved in promoting the development of many new services such as mental health services, the deaf outreach project for AIDS patients, the first literacy and life skills program and the telephone relay service. This was all on top of his work as a Vocational Rehab counselor. I think it was around the mid-1980's when Gary really bloomed. He rose to the occasion, if you will.....The government was proposing to do away with the residential deaf schools and to mainstream all deaf kids. Gary got interested in meeting parent groups and promoting a bilingual/bicultural approach to deaf education. Do you remember what happened when you met with the parents who supported the Total Communication approach?

GARY
(*Smiling.*)

YES, YES.

IRIS

Here were the parents who had fought hard to get some sign language into the schools and they were constantly battling the voice parents. So he comes into a meeting and blasts them! What did you tell them?

GARY
(*Laughing.*)

THE TRUTH! SIM-COM IS WRONG. ASL IS RIGHT!

IRIS

So these parents are feeling terrible, slinking down in their chairs. One father started arguing with Gary. So when it was over, I took Gary aside....(*To GARY.*) This is not the way to win people over! You can't tell them they're wrong. Things they've invested in.

GARY

BUT IT'S WRONG. IT SHOULDN'T BE THIS WAY. THEY DON'T UNDERSTAND.

IRIS

So how are we going to make them understand? What should we do?

Enters JUDY REBICK, *a middle-aged woman wearing jeans, a T-shirt and sandals.*

GARY

I DON'T KNOW.

IRIS

Let's ask Judy....
(*To the audience.*)

Judy Rebick was a social activist, a feminist, an abortion-rights advocate, and in a few years time would become the leader of Canada's National Action Committee on the Status of Women.

GARY

SHE WAS A BIG TIME SHIT-KICKER!

IRIS

Yes, and she worked at CHS, too

GARY

SHE REALLY OPENED DOORS FOR ME.

JUDY REBICK
(*Signing and voicing to the audience.*)

I met Gary when he started working at the Canadian Hearing Society. He seemed to have an interest in advocacy and politics. Since I was in charge of advocacy and there were few deaf staff who seemed at all interested in politics, I immediately began spending time with Gary. Some people thought he had a chip on his shoulder. I had quite a different attitude. As a political person who had been working with deaf people for many years with some level of frustration, I immediately saw the leadership potential in Gary and was really excited about him.

IRIS

So Judy?

JUDY

Yes?

IRIS

We're stuck. We've got a group of parents with deaf kids who are supportive of some instruction in sign language. However, we all know that for most deaf kids it would be better if all their classes were in ASL, how do we get the parents to support this?

JUDY
Well, I don't think you are going to get the whole hog until you have something to back it up...like research. We need to show people the proof that it's better for deaf kids to be educated in a language where everything is clear and there's no guess work involved and where they can express themselves easily and completely. Do you have any research to show that?

GARY
NO. I WILL FIND SOME.

NARRATOR
While things were going well in Gary's professional life, his personal life was starting to fall apart.

Lights out on the CHS office setting and up on a small apartment living room where MARY *stands as* GARY *walks into the scene.*

GARY
(*As he enters.*)

HI.

MARY
HI. WE NEED TO TALK.

GARY
WHY? WHAT'S UP?

MARY

I FEEL LIKE A SINGLE MOM.   YOU'RE
NEVER HOME.

GARY

I'M BUSY. THERE'S SO MUCH TO DO.

MARY

I KNOW YOUR WORK IS IMPORTANT TO
YOU.   AND   I   KNOW   THE   ONTARIO
ASSOCIATION OF THE DEAF IS IMPORTANT
TOO. BUT WHAT ABOUT YOUR WIFE AND
TWO KIDS?

GARY
(*Defensively.*)

YOU AND THE KIDS ARE IMPORTANT TO
ME.

MARY

THEN WHY DON'T YOU SPEND TIME WITH
US? EVERYDAY YOU LEAVE FIRST THING
IN THE MORNING AND YOU COME HOME
LATE AT NIGHT. AND ON WEEKENDS YOU
ARE GONE FREQUENTLY ALSO.

GARY

YES, I KNOW. I WILL TRY TO BE HERE
MORE.

MARY

I NEED TIME FOR MYSELF TOO.

GARY

YES, YOU NEED TO MAKE FRIENDS AND GO OUT MORE, I AGREE.

MARY

AND WE NEED MORE TIME TOGETHER. DON'T YOU WANT TO BE WITH ME?

GARY

YES, BUT THERE'S SO MUCH TO DO AND YOU DON'T SEEM TO WANT TO BE INVOLVED.

MARY

WELL, I'M NOT AN ACTIVIST LIKE YOU...I JUST WANT TO GO OUT WITH FRIENDS AND WITH OTHER FAMILIES.

GARY

WE DO THAT!

MARY

I KNOW SOMETIMES BUT IT IS NOT VERY OFTEN. I AM SO LONELY HERE.

GARY

I KNOW. I AM SORRY.

MARY

I MISS MY FRIENDS AND MY FAMILY. I WANT TO GO BACK TO MARYLAND OR NEW JERSEY.

GARY

BUT I HAVE A GOOD JOB HERE AND
CANADA IS SO MUCH SAFER. MAYBE WE
CAN VISIT YOUR FAMILY MORE OFTEN.

MARY

I NEED TO BE WITH YOU MORE OFTEN.

GARY

I SAID I WOULD TRY.....

MARY

CAN I ASK YOU SOMETHING?

GARY

SURE.

MARY

WILL YOU ANSWER ME HONEST?

GARY

YES.

MARY

DO YOU STILL LOVE ME? TRULY, DO YOU
LOVE ME?

GARY
(*Mouth drops open.*)

WHAT?!

MARY

DO YOU LOVE ME STILL?

GARY
(*After a moment.*)

I DON'T KNOW.

MARY

DON'T LIE TO ME. TELL ME.

GARY

THIS IS NOT A GOOD TIME TO TALK. IT IS
LATE. YOU ARE TIRED AND I AM TIRED.

MARY

TELL ME NOW! DO YOU LOVE ME?

GARY
(*Resigned.*)

NO.

MARY
(*As if slapped, she bursts into
tears.*)

I KNEW, I KNEW.

GARY

I AM SORRY.

MARY *falls into a chair and cries with her face in her
hands.* GARY, *feeling awful, slumps beside her and rubs
her back. After a few moments,* MARY *raises her head.*

MARY

I WILL MOVE BACK TO NEW JERSEY AFTER
THE BABY IS BORN.

GARY
(*Shocked.*)

BABY?

MARY
I AM TWO MONTHS PREGNANT.

GARY
OH. WOW.

MARY
I AM SORRY. I KNOW YOU WANTED TO WAIT.

GARY
YES, I THOUGHT WE AGREED.

MARY
I KNOW. I THOUGHT IT WOULD BE GOOD FOR US.

GARY
WELL....I DON'T KNOW WHAT TO SAY.

MARY
YOU DON'T HAVE TO SAY ANYTHING. MY MOM WILL HELP ME WITH THE BABY.

GARY
WHAT ARE YOU SAYING? WE HAVE TO STAY TOGETHER. WE CAN STILL BE A FAMILY.

MARY
(*Crying again.*)
WE CAN'T IF YOU DON'T LOVE ME.

GARY

WAIT, WAIT, WAIT. LET'S GO TO A COUNSELOR, YOU KNOW, A MARRIAGE COUNSELOR.

MARY

FINE. BUT I DON'T THINK IT'S GOING TO CHANGE ANYTHING IF YOU DON'T LOVE. ME.

Lights slow fade out on the scene as a spotlight comes up on GARY.

GARY
(*To the audience.*)
I BROKE MARY'S HEART THAT NIGHT. WE WENT TO A MARRIAGE COUNSELOR FOR AWHILE BUT IT DIDN'T HELP. I FOUND OUT I REALLY HAD A PROBLEM. I HAD THIS "SO WHAT" ATTITUDE. I WASN'T VERY CONSIDERATE OF PEOPLE'S FEELINGS. I SHOULDN'T HAVE GOTTEN MARRIED.
(*A heavy sigh.*)
JULY 3, 1987 WAS THE OFFICIAL DAY OF SEPARATION. I DROVE MARY AND THE GIRLS TO NEW JERSEY. CARLEE WAS 5 YEARS OLD, SARA WAS 18 MONTHS OLD AND MARISSA WAS 6 MONTHS OLD.

(Pause and heavy sigh.)

I DIDN'T KNOW WHAT WAS GOING TO HAPPEN WITH THE SEPARATION PROCESS. I REMEMBER LOADING UP THE CAR AND DRIVING TO NEW JERSEY. I REMEMBER TELLING CARLEE, "I WILL COME BACK AND SEE YOU ON YOUR BIRTHDAY."
SHE SAID, "WHAT?!" SHE CRIED AND CRIED AND CRIED. SHE KNEW. SHE HAD FIGURED IT OUT. IT WAS BAD.

(Pause. Looks away for a moment.)

OH, BOY, DID I FEEL GUILTY WHEN I DROVE BACK TO ONTARIO. I CRIED AND CRIED AND CRIED. "WHY DID I DO THIS?! WHAT A MESS! I NEVER SHOULD HAVE PUT THESE CHILDREN THROUGH THIS EXPERIENCE."

(Pause.)

I TRIED TO GET BACK AS OFTEN AS I COULD. I WENT TO NEW JERSEY EVERY MONTH. IT WAS HARD ACCEPTING THE SEPARATION. I ASKED MARY TO COME BACK TO TORONTO BUT SHE SAID NO. WE HAD SOME BAD DISCUSSIONS ABOUT THAT. I WAS ANGRY AND FRUSTRATED, SO I KEPT MYSELF BUSY WITH THE DEAF COMMUNITY. I WANTED TO AVOID MY FEELINGS, SO I DOVE INTO MY WORK. MY ADVOCACY.

Lights fade out on GARY *and come up on* IRIS, JUDY *and* DENIS.

IRIS

(*Signing and speaking.*)

Probably one of the most important things Gary did at CHS was getting Denis to hire Patty Shores. The two of them were a great one-two punch.

JUDY

When Gary first came to CHS, he was very angry. He had very little to do with hearing people. I thought it was justifiable rage. The deaf were oppressed in every way: linguistically, economically and socially and they just accepted it. Gary was one of the first to come along who wouldn't accept it. Then there was Patty. Gary was good at community development. Patty's strength was that she was very charming and could communicate with hearing people. Gary is a lot of things, but "charming" is not one of them. He learned to communicate with hearing people when he saw that it was useful. Patty was a better spokesperson. The made a good team.

IRIS

Yes, they worked wonderfully together. Patty was definitely diplomatic and a politician. She was a very good influence on him.

DENIS

When they met with hearing people, bureaucrats and politicians, they would just blow them away.

PATTY

(*Entering and signing.*)

GARY IS THE SAME AS HE WAS AT GALLAUDET. HE IS VERY BUSY. HE MUST

ALWAYS BE DOING SOMETHING. GARY ENCOURAGED ME TO TAKE A JOB AT CHS. HE WANTED US TO WORK TOGETHER ON COMMUNITY DEVELOPMENT. HIS CUBICLE WAS NEAR MINE AND HE WAS ALWAYS POPPING OVER TO TELL ME SOMETHING ABOUT WHAT THE GOVERNMENT WAS DOING. HE GOT ME INVOLVED IN THE ONTARIO ASSOCIATION FOR THE DEAF'S EDUCATIONAL TASK FORCE. THEN MARCH, 1988 CAME ALONG AND SOMETHING BIG HAPPENED AT GALLAUDET TO REALLY ENCOURAGE US.

GARY *enters.*

GARY

DEAF PRESIDENT NOW! DEAF PRESIDENT NOW!! DEAF PRESIDENT NOW!!!

IRIS, JUDY, KAREN *and* DENIS *applaud* GARY.

PATTY

THE GALLAUDET REVOLUTION! IT WAS A HUGE STEP FOR DEAF PEOPLE. WE WERE ALL EXCITED.

GARY
(Marching around.)

DEAF PRESIDENT NOW! DEAF PRESIDENT NOW!
DEAF PRESIDENT NOW!

PATTY
(*Marching now too.*)

WE REALIZED WE COULD CHANGE THE
WORLD.

GARY
(*Still marching.*)

DEAF ONTARIO NOW! DEAF ONTARIO
NOW!! DEAF ONTARIO NOW!!!

PATTY

WE CHANGED THE NAME OF OUR DEAF
EDUCATIONAL REVIEW MOVEMENT TO
DEAF ONTARIO NOW.

GARY

THE SPIRIT OF DEAF PRESIDENT NOW
INSPIRED, EMPOWERED AND ENERGIZED
US.

JUDY
(*To the audience.*)

Gary was very interested in politics but he had very
little contact with the hearing world of politics. He
and Patty sought my advice....

JUDY *sits down behind a desk and* PATTY *and* GARY
approach her.

GARY

WE NEED YOU HELP. WE WANT TO
DEVELOP A STRATEGY FOR REFORMING
DEAF EDUCATION.

71

PATTY

WE WANT TO GET BILINGUAL AND
BICULTURAL EDUCATION INTO THE
PROVINCIAL DEAF SCHOOLS.

JUDY

Okay. That's not going to be quick and easy. We
need to start with a simple demand that can be won.

GARY

WOLLASTON OUT!

JUDY

(*To the audience.*)

At the time, Roy Wollaston was in charge of deaf
education for the province of Ontario.

GARY

WOLLASTON IS A NICE MAN WHO GIVES
BORING SPEECHES BUT HIS ATTITUDE
TOWARDS DEAF PEOPLE IS PATERNALISTIC
AND OPPRESSIVE.

JUDY

Getting rid of Wollaston might take a really long
time and that's just going to get everyone on the
defensive.

PATTY

WELL, WHAT SHOULD WE DO THEN?

JUDY

Why not demand a review of deaf education in the
province of Ontario? You can't just force people to
change, somehow we need to show what is

currently happening and then look at the research. And show why a change is necessary.

GARY

HOW DO WE DO THAT?

JUDY

We need to meet with Richard Johnston.

GARY

WHO'S HE?

JUDY

He's a member of provincial parliament from Scarborough. He's the education critic for the New Democratic Party. He can help us get the provincial government's attention. If we convince him, he can introduce a member's bill to the legislature....Do you want to meet him?

GARY

SURE. WHY NOT?

JUDY

Okay, I'll set it up.

They cross into RICHARD JOHNSTON's *office. He is a middle-aged and dressed casually in a coat and tie.*

JUDY

Richard, this is Patty Shores-Hermann and Gary Malkowski

73

RICHARD
(*Stands and shakes their hands, while* JUDY *serves as interpreter.*)

Nice to meet you. Thank you for coming to see me. Judy has informed me of the issues with deaf education in the province and that you have met with the Ministry.

GARY & JUDY
Yes, we met with Roy Wollaston.

RICHARD
And how did it go?

GARY & JUDY
We are disgusted with his answers.

PATTY & JUDY
We have learned that the Ministry has no policies, no recommendations about how the special schools should be run. It was up to each superintendent to run their schools as they saw fit.

RICHARD
So they have no formal mechanism for running the schools?

GARY & JUDY
Yes.

RICHARD
And what do you want to do about this?

PATTY & JUDY
We want a public inquiry.

GARY & JUDY

And we want to sue the Ontario government for negligence.

JUDY

I told them they're nuts. These are unrealistic demands. What do you think?

RICHARD

Let's go for it. Let's give it a shot.

JUDY

Seriously?

GARY & JUDY

So you are going to help us?

RICHARD

Yes, if you let me join you. I need a new cause. This is my last year in the legislature. I'm retiring and I've been looking to introduce a private member's bill. This is a fight for accessibility and I can see the oppression your community has experienced. I want to help. As a socialist this grabs me. So let's sit down and hammer this out....

As the four move to sit down, the lights fade out and a spotlight comes up on GARY.

GARY

(*To the audience.*)

ON MAY 5, 1988 RICHARD JONHSTON STOOD UP IN THE ONTARIO PROVINCIAL PARLIAMENT AND INTRODUCED A PRIVATE MEMBER'S RESOLUTION CALLING

FOR A MAJOR OVERHAUL OF PROVINCIAL POLICIES AND PRACTICES CONCERNING THE EDUCATION OF DEAF PEOPLE IN ONTARIO. A BUNCH OF US WERE IN THE BALCONY OVERLOOKING THE CHAMBER....

Lights up on RICHARD *centerstage as* GARY, PATTY, JUDY, IRIS, DENIS *and others move up a couple of levels so that they are looking down on the politician.* DEAN WILL *serves as the interpreter.*

RICHARD
(Signing, stiffly.)

GOOD MORNING, I AM GOING TO TALK ABOUT THE DEAF.

GARY
(Proudly, to those around him.)

I TAUGHT HIM THAT.

RICHARD
(Speaking to audience.)

I wish that today in this Legislature a deaf person could be standing here and speaking to members in sign language. That unfortunately is not possible because of the total disempowerment, disfranchisement of those people over the generations, especially through the poor education that we have given them in Ontario and other jurisdictions across Canada. There are today in the House a number of people who are deaf. They are coming, as people have come recently from Gallaudet College in Washington, to say that the silence has gone on long enough, that Deaf people must be heard as they choose to be heard. Their rights to determine their education and the way they should be taught in the province is paramount. There is no longer time for us to get in their way.

(*Pausing and looking up to the Deaf supporters, who are applauding.*)

I have only recently come to this issue, but I am totally consumed by it now. I have been reading the history of the systematic and systemic discrimination against the deaf that has gone on for more than 100 years and the role of even great men like Alexander Graham Bell in suppressing the rights of the Deaf. Members may not know that he was in fact a major spokesman at the turn of the century against the rights of Deaf people to intermarry, because he wanted to stop the supposed genetic carrying on of deafness. He worked very hard against the rights of the Deaf. Back before the turn of the century, the deaf were taught in sign language and many of the teachers were deaf themselves. Now, there are 170 teachers of the deaf in Ontario and only 8 are hearing impaired. And the provincial schools are using different forms of sign language, trying to put English on hands, and excluding ASL, the language that most deaf people prefer. And there are enormous problems for hearing-impaired students who are mainstreamed without the support of ASL interpreters. It's time we stood up and did something about these problems. The deaf are not going to be quiet about these issues any longer. The Deaf are not going to sit idly by and allow this discrimination and limited opportunities to continue.

The Deaf supporters applaud wildly and hoot. RICHARD *looks up and give them a thumbs up. Light out and spot up on* GARY.

GARY

AFTER RICHARD'S SPEECH, WE HELD A PRESS CONFERENCE AND SINCE I WAS CHAIRMAN OF THE EDUCATION TASK FORCE OF THE ONTARIO ASSOCIATION OF THE DEAF, I WAS INTERVIEWED BY THE MEDIA. I SAID, "WE SUPPORT BILINGUAL EDUCATION. WE WANT DEAF CHILDREN TO LEARN BASIC SKILLS IN BOTH ASL AND ENGLISH. WE SUPPORT A WELL-ROUNDED EDUCATION AND WE WANT MORE INPUT. WE HAVE NEVER BEEN INVITED TO PARTICIPATE IN THE PROCESS BY THE MINISTER OF EDUCATION AND WE'RE NOT GOING TO WAIT ANY LONGER. IT'S TIME HE STARTED LISTENING. THE STUDENTS OF GALLAUDET HAVE TAKEN CONTROL OF THEIR OWN DESTINY. LIKE THEM, WE'VE HAD ENOUGH OF BEING PUPPETS WITH HEARING PEOPLE AT THE STRINGS."

(Pause.)

I GUESS YOU COULD SAY THIS WAS THE BEGINNING OF MY POLITICAL CAREER.

(Marching off.)

DEAF ONTARIO NOW! DEAF ONTARIO NOW! DEAF ONTARIO NOW!

Lights up on an office setting where there are three or four desks grouped together. KAREN is sitting at one of the desks doing paperwork when GARY enters.

KAREN

(Putting down her work.)

Hey, how did it go at Queen's Park?

GARY

PRETTY GOOD. RICHARD'S SPEECH WAS GOOD AND MANY MEMBERS SUPPORTED THE RESOLUTION.

KAREN

Wonderful.

GARY

AT THE PRESS CONFERENCE, I WAS INTERVIEWED BY NEWSPAPER WRITERS AND TELEVISION REPORTERS.

KAREN

Really?!

GARY

YEAH! I'M GOING TO BE ON THE CBC NEWS TONIGHT.

KAREN

Wow! You're becoming a media star.

GARY

HEY, HAVE YOU EATEN YET?

KAREN

No.

GARY

DO YOU WANT TO GO OUT AND HAVE DINNER SOMEWHERE?

KAREN

Are you asking me out?

GARY

I DON'T KNOW. YEAH, I GUESS SO.

KAREN

What happened to the guy who told me a year ago that he would never date a hearing woman?

GARY

WHO SAID THAT?

KAREN

Mr. Deaf Culture Media Star said that.

GARY

(*Shrugs and laughs.*)

WHO'S THAT?

KAREN

(*Laughing.*)

You are!

GARY

SOMETIMES I SAY STUPID THINGS.

KAREN

Maybe asking me out is one of those stupid things?

GARY

NOOOOO! COME ON, LET'S GO GET SOME PIZZA AT GINO'S RESTAURANT.

KAREN

Gino's?!!! They won't serve us there. You have a lawsuit against them, don't you?

GARY

YES. BUT THEY DON'T DISCRIMINATE
AGAINST DEAF PEOPLE NOW.

KAREN

So they settled the case?

GARY

NOT YET, BUT THEY DON'T WANT
ANOTHER INCIDENT OR TO BE SUED
AGAIN. COME ON, LET'S GO, THEY WILL
GIVE US GOOD SERVICE NOW.

KAREN

Oh, sure. (*Laughing.*) They'll probably spit on our
pizza.

GARY
(*Laughing.*)

NOOOOO!

KAREN

Well, I don't know about this. I've never gone out
with a deaf guy before.

GARY

I HAVE NEVER DATED A HEARING WOMAN
BEFORE.

KAREN

Aren't you worried about what your friends are
going to say?

GARY

NOOOO!

KAREN

Well, I am worried what our co-workers are going to say.

GARY

WHO CARES WHAT THEY SAY?

KAREN

No, we have to think about this. It might not be good for us to date. I mean, we work right next to each other...If it didn't go well, you know, there could be some hard feelings. And—

GARY

NOOO!!!

KAREN

YESSSSS!!!

GARY

IT'S NOT A BIG DEAL. WE'RE JUST GOING OUT FOR SOME PIZZA. WE'RE COLLEAGUES AND WE'LL TALK ABOUT WORK. COME ON, I WANT TO TELL YOU WHAT DEAF ONTARIO NOW HAS PLANNED. WE'RE GOING TO ORGANIZE SOME RALLIES AND PROTESTS AND MAYBE A SIT-IN OF THE MINISTRY OF EDUCATION'S OFFICE.

KAREN

Wow! Really?

GARY

YEAH, COME ON...

GARY *grabs* KAREN's *coat off and holds it open for her to slide into.* KAREN *looks at him for a moment, smiles and puts on her coat with* GARY's *help. They start to walk off.*

GARY

SO WHAT DO YOU LIKE ON YOUR PIZZA? PEPPERONI? MUSHROOMS?

KAREN

Anything but spit!

GARY *and* KAREN *laugh as they move upstage.* IRIS *enters from downstage left and* DENIS *enters from downstage right and* PATTY *enters from upstage opposite of where* GARY *and* KAREN *stand.*

IRIS

There was a lot of gossip around CHS about Gary and Karen. I didn't believe any of it. I remember they both had their cars parked near mine and I would be leaving and there were Karen and Gary in the parking lot always chatting. And then these rumors would start and I would say, "That's ridiculous! Why do people have to always think it's a romance?! They're colleagues, they're just talking, for God's sake!" And then I found out it was true! I was surprised that they were a couple.

DENIS

Hearing people who dealt with Karen professionally were shocked to learn about Karen and Gary. They saw Karen as being so nice and Gary being this Deaf Power guy! It was shocking to them.

PATTY

KAREN AND GARY WENT TO DEAF SOCIAL EVENTS TOGETHER. WE DEAF PEOPLE TALKED ABOUT IT, BUT THERE WASN'T A PROBLEM. THEY BOTH HAD SUCH POSITIVE ATTITUDES. DEAF PEOPLE KNEW KAREN LONG BEFORE GARY FORMED A RELATIONSHIP WITH HER. WE LIKED KAREN. I DON'T THINK ANYONE EVER WENT UP TO GARY AND SAID, "DON'T DATE KAREN, SHE'S HEARING!"

KAREN
(As she enters, the others exit.)

I never thought it would go beyond dating. I couldn't image us together. A typical date was for us to go to the Carlton Cinema and see foreign films, which were open-captioned. Gary and I went out together for over a year before we moved into together. It wasn't a big adjustment. He was away often with community meetings and visiting his girls in New Jersey. It was tough for him when he came back. He would be depressed and in tears. I don't know how he could stand it, but we'd go out and do something to cheer him up.

Gary was quiet and peaceful. I liked that I could play my music any time and Gary could watch sports on TV with the volume turned down. In the beginning, when I wasn't fluent in ASL, I did feel pressure. Gary was much more confident that we could overcome the cultural issues than I was. It helped that we are confident in our identities. I don't pretend to be deaf or have ASL equal to my English. I think the Deaf Community sees us trying hard to integrate and show respect for both cultures.

GARY

KAREN WAS THE BEST THING THAT EVER HAPPENED TO ME.   I COULDN'T HAVE DONE ANY OF THE ACCOMPLISHMENTS THAT HAPPENED WITHOUT HER SUPPORT AND LOVE.

(They kiss and hug.)

Lights out on the scene and spotlight on the NARRATOR.

NARRATOR
(To the audience.)

Come back in fifteen minutes and we'll show how Gary became an elected politician.

Lights out.

End of Act One.

Richard Medugno

ACT TWO:

Opens with a spotlight on the NARRATOR.

NARRATOR

In the late 1980's, under Gary Malkowski's guidance a coalition was created in Ontario and it was called the Education Task Force. It included every party that had a stake in deaf education in the province. Gary played a tremendous role bringing all the groups together: parents, the Ministry of Education, the deaf groups. Gary helped with the negotiating that brought them all together. He had to play both sides of the fence to get the parents who opposed sign language to trust that the Deaf were just trying to do what they thought was right. And he got his own group, the Ontario Association of the Deaf, to come along too. He said to them, "If you're not going to listen to the oral parent group, why should they listen to us? And if we don't listen to one another, where does that get us? Nowhere!"

Spotlight on JUDY.

JUDY

The Liberal government agreed to implement a review on deaf education because there hadn't been one in the province for twenty years.

Spotlight on GARY.

GARY

SO THE MINISTER OF EDUCATION TOLD US THE REVIEW AND RECOMMENDATIONS WERE GOING TO BE COMPLETED IN THE

SUMMER OF 1989. WE CONTINUED TO APPLY POLITICAL PRESSURE TO ENSURE THAT THE REVIEW ITSELF WOULD BE CONDUCTED IN AN EQUITABLE MANNER. THE BATTLE WAS BETWEEN TWO DIFFERENT APPROACHES. ONE GROUP SAW HEARING LOSS AS A HANDICAP IN NEED OF A CURE, EMPHASIZING ORAL SKILLS AND AUDIO AIDS. THIS GROUP REJECTED DEAF CULTURE AND REGARDS A NORMAL HEARING PERSON AS A ROLE MODEL. THE OTHER GROUP—THE DEAF COMMUNITY EMPHASIZES ABILITY NOT DISABILITY, ENCOURAGES DEVELOPMENT OF ALL COMMUNICATION MODES AND USES SUCCESSFUL DEAF ADULTS AS ROLE MODELS. WHAT GROUP DID I BELONG TO? I AM PROUD TO BE DEAF. I HAVE NOTHING TO BE ASHAMED OF. HEARING PEOPLE CAN'T BE ALLOWED TO CONTROL OUR LIVES BECAUSE THEY CAN'T UNDERSTAND OUR NEEDS. AS A COMMUNITY WE WERE FIGHTING FOR IMPROVED SERVICES AND WE WERE LOSING OUR PATIENCE.

JUDY

The minister promised the review reports would be released to the public in the summer of 1989, but summer came and went and they didn't do it. Then they promised they would by early fall and then late fall. The Deaf community wasn't going to wait and patiently sit on their hands while the review kept getting delayed...

GARY

ON DECEMBER 14, I SENT THE MINISTER OF
EDUCATION A LETTER SAYING THAT WE
ARE TIRED OF HIS BROKEN PROMISES AND
THE STALLING AND HIS REFUSAL TO MEET
WITH US. I DIDN'T EXPECT ANY RESPONSE.
THE NEXT MORNING WE STAGED A SIT-IN
OF HIS OFFICE AT THE EDUCATION
MINISTRY.

Lights up on the Education Ministry office. Two middle-aged women, SECRETARIES, *sit behind a couple of desks typing.*

DEAN WILL *enters.*

DEAN

Hello.

SECRETARY #1
(*Still typing.*)

May I help you?

DEAN

Yes. I'm the sign language interpreter. I'm here
for Gary Malkowski's meeting with the Minister of
Education.

SECRETARY #1
(*Stops typing and looks up.*)

The Minister is not here....(*Checking a
calendar.*)...And there's nothing on his schedule—

Suddenly, lead by GARY, *a group of deaf people burst onto
the scene carrying protest signs that read "Deaf Ed Review*

*Report Now!", "Deaf Schools Now!", "Deaf Ontario Now"
and "Deaf Teachers Now".*

DEAF PROTESTERS
(*Marching in a big circle around the desks.*)
NOW, NOW, NOW, STOP THE BULLSHIT!
NOW, NOW, NOW, STOP THE BULLSHIT!

SECRETARY #1
What the—You people can't come in here....What
are they saying?

DEAN
Stop the bullshit now.

SECRETARY #2
(*Picking up a phone.*)
This is the Ministry of Education office, we need
security here.   Now.....We have a bunch of
protesters disrupting...You can't hear anything
because they're deaf. It may be quiet but they are
disturbing   us.....The   protesters   are   deaf
people.....No, not dead people, deaf! D-E-A-F!!

As the marching and chatting continues, GARY *grabs*
DEAN *and they come down to* SECRETARY #1, *with*
DEAN *voicing for* GARY.

GARY & DEAN
I demand a meeting with the Minister.

SECRETARY #1
He's not here.

GARY & DEAN

Someone better call him because we are not leaving until we meet with him.

SECRETARY #1

Oh, my God, this is ridiculous....

As the SECRETARY *gets on the phone, a* CAMERAMAN *and* REPORTER #1 *come into the office, along with a photographer who begins to shoot pictures of the scene.* GARY *poses for one shot, holding up his sign with the irritated* SECRETARY *in the background grimacing.*

REPORTER #1

What's this protest all about?

GARY & DEAN

It's about broken promises and the Minister of Education sitting on a Deaf Education report. If he does not release it soon, another school year can go by without implementing the recommendations and deaf children will continue to suffer.

GARY *rejoins the protesters march and the "Now, Now, Now, Stop the Bullshit" chant.*

REPORTER #1

What are they signing?

DEAN

They're all chanting, "Now, Now, Now, Stop the Bullshit."

REPORTER #1
(*To the cameraman.*)
Okay, we're going to have to edit that out.

SECRETARY #1
(*Yelling to anyone who will listen.*)
Okay! The Minister's senior aide is coming over!

GARY
(*After DEAN has relayed the message.*)
THANK YOU.

The lights fade out as a spotlight come on the REPORTER #1 *who is speaking into the TV camera, while* DEAN *interprets what she is saying for the deaf.*

REPORTER #1
...The sit-in at the Ministry of Education office began at 10 a.m. when 30 to 40 deaf protesters from the Ontario Association of the Deaf filled the lobby, demanding a meeting with the Minister and the release of a long overdue report on the quality of deaf education in the province of Ontario. The leader of the deaf group Gary Malkowski informed us through a sign language interpreter that the protesters planned to occupy the office until they met with the minister. It looked as if the police might have to be called in to remove the protesters until the Minister's senior aide arrived and via a long-distance call with the minister who is back in his home in Northern Ontario, hammered out a written commitment to meet the main demand of the protesters. The minister agreed to release the report in the provincial parliament on December 20,

1989. From Queen's Park, this is the CBC Evening News....

Lights out on the REPORTER #1 *and spotlight up on* GARY.

GARY

THE SIT-IN WAS A HUGE VICTORY. IT TOOK A LOT MORE ADVOCACY AND PROTESTING AND LOBBYING. IT TOOK A FEW YEARS, BUT MOST OF THE RECOMMEDATIONS MADE IN THE DEAF EDUCATION REVIEW WERE IMPLEMENTED, SUCH AS ASL AS A LANGUAGE OF INSTRUCTION, HIIRING DEAΓ ADMINISTRATORS AND DEAF TEACHERS, AND CREATING THE TEACHER OF THE DEAF TRAINING PROGRAMS AND THE PERMANENT ADVISORY COMMITTEE TO THE MINISTER OF EDUCATION. PAH!

Lights out on GARY *and up on* RICHARD JOHNSTON *in his office. He is sitting behind a chair.*

RICHARD JOHNSTON

For my last act as a member of provincial parliament, I introduced a private member's bill to make American Sign Language and *Langue des signes quebecois* as languages of instruction and heritage languages in Ontario. We got it through two readings in the legislature with nearly unanimous approval and all we needed was for the premier to sign it and it would have become law. But instead, the premier called an election and the bill died...But the call for the election gave birth to something new, something great. Something that's never happened before. The election of a deaf man to a senior government position....It all started in my office one spring morning in 1990, when Gary came to see me to discuss how the bill might still be saved....I was reading the *Toronto Star* newspaper when he arrived....

RICHARD *cracks open a newspaper and begins reading. A few moments later,* GARY *and* JUDY *enter.*

GARY
GOOD MORNING!

JUDY
Hello, Richard.

RICHARD
Hello, Hello....Hey, did you see this....?

JUDY *signs for* RICHARD *and voices for* GARY.

JUDY
What is it?

RICHARD
Christine Hart's resigned her cabinet position...

(Reading the newspaper.)

"York East M.P.P. Christine Hart has quit the Ontario provincial cabinet as Minister of Culture yesterday after admitting she accepted political help from employees of two communication companies...The premier says there was nothing illegal, but he was concerned about the potential conflict of interest...."

GARY & JUDY

I live in East York. She's my M.P.P.!

RICHARD

She is going to be vulnerable in the election....
(Joking.)
Hey, Gary, why don't you run for her seat?

GARY & JUDY
(Seriously.)
You think I should be a candidate?

RICHARD
(His smile disappearing.)
Ah....Well, they do need an New Democratic Party
candidate for that riding...

GARY & JUDY

You think I could be a Member of Provincial
Parliament?

RICHARD

Sure. You'd be terrific. I have always thought in
the past that it would be great to have candidates
who were disabled or disadvantaged.

GARY & JUDY

Okay, what's the procedure? How do I get
involved? How do I run for office?

RICHARD

You really want to run?

GARY

Yes!

RICHARD

Don't you want to think about it?

GARY & JUDY
(*Shrugs*.)

No. I really want to try. How do I get started?

RICHARD

Well, are you a member of any political party?

GARY & JUDY

Well, to tell you the truth, I don't even know the differences between the parties.

RICHARD

Oh, come on. You're doing what a social democrat would do. You would fit in with the New Democratic Party. Here, let's get you signed up.

RICHARD *pulls a form out from his desk and starts to fill in some of the form.*

RICHARD

Just sign here.....

GARY *takes a pen and signs the form. He returns the form to* RICHARD.

RICHARD

Are you sure you want to be a politician?

GARY

Yes!

RICHARD

Are you sure you want to be an M.P.P.? It's a big challenge and it could lead to a hectic life. It would really cut into your family time.

GARY & JUDY

I want to try. I know I am a long-shot but I want to try anyway.

RICHARD

Great. This is going to be fun.
(They shake hands.)

Spotlight on the NARRATOR.

NARRATOR

A couple of weeks after Gary decided to run for office, Richard Johnston introduced him to the York East Riding Association for the New Democratic Party. This was the local political organization that would help Gary run for office.

Spotlight up on RICHARD JOHNSTON.

RICHARD

After Gary decided he wanted to run, I contacted the riding association and they were not enthusiastic about having a deaf candidate. I didn't have much power to twist arms with, but I tried to cajole and convince them Gary would be a great candidate. They were reluctant but they were having trouble fielding candidates. It was a really moribund organization. They had a loser lethargy. No one wanted to run and finish a distant third. I explained Gary's history and what a passionate hard worker he was and how it would be historic. Finally, they saw that having a candidate like Gary on their behalf had a lot of upside. So they agreed, but no one, myself included, had any expectations that he could possibly win a seat. A lot of folks running the Ontario NDP thought it was a "neat" idea, but the party wasn't really ready for the implications of having a deaf candidate, like the costs of interpreters....

Spotlight out on RICHARD.

NARRATOR

Here's a little background on the politics of the province of Ontario at the time. There were three major parties: the Conservatives, who had run the provincial government for years until the last election when the Liberal party had won. For the past five years, the Liberals had enjoyed pretty good support and called an election as they are able to do in a parliamentary government, when they felt they had the best chance of getting re-elected. The New Democratic Party, also known as the NDP, was the third major party, a socialist group that had been on the outside, close to a fringe party, for years. They did have a young, bright, charismatic leader named Bob Rae. He loved the idea of having a disabled candidate on his party's ticket. A few weeks after Gary's candidacy was brought up, Bob Rae visited Malkowski at his office at the Canadian Hearing Society.

Lights up on GARY *sitting at his desk working on some papers, when* JUDY *enters with* BOB RAE *at her side.*

JUDY *serves as interpreter. As the scene, progresses* DENIS, IRIS *and* KAREN *and maybe a few other co-workers enter and observe the meeting.*

JUDY

Bob Rae is here to see you.

BOB RAE

Gary, it's a pleasure to meet you.

GARY & JUDY
(*Stands up, a little awed.*)

Nice to meet you.

The men shake hands.

BOB RAE

Sorry to bother you at work, but I just wanted to come down and meet you.

GARY & JUDY

Thank you for coming.

BOB RAE

I also wanted you to know I'm delighted you are considering running as an NDP candidate. We really need more people like you—advocates from the community involved in the political process.

GARY & JUDY

So you support me running for office?

BOB RAE

Absolutely. I promise you'll get the full support of the Ontario NDP. The York East riding is wide

open.   You have a good chance at defeating
Christine Hart.   She's vulnerable since she had to
resign from the cabinet.

GARY & JUDY

You think I have a chance to win?

BOB RAE

Sure, it's possible. If you and the riding association
work hard, we might be able to upset a few apple
carts.

GARY & JUDY

Okay! Great!! What happens now?

BOB RAE

We'll get the riding association to set up a
nomination meeting and I will come and speak on
your behalf. We'll get the media there to cover the
whole thing. I'm sure they'll be very interested in
your candidacy.   Do you know of any other
hearing-impaired candidates?

GARY & JUDY

No. I have never heard of any deaf person running
for public office. (*Turning to his colleagues.*) Have
any of you?

(*They all shake their heads "no".*)

I guess I will be the first.

BOB RAE

Fantastic. Listen, Gary, you may not win in
September, but that's not what's important. What is
important is that you break new ground here and get
people's attention and get our agenda out there. It's

going to take some time, but when the public starts to realize that we're the kind of party that supports the disabled, they'll join us and we'll be able to change the system.

GARY *smiles as his colleagues applaud. Some start to chant "DEAF ONTARIO NOW, DEAF ONTARIO NOW." Lights out on the scene and spotlight up on* JAMES.

JAMES
GARY WAS VERY EXCITED WHEN HE CALLED ME TO SAY THAT HE WOULD BE RUNNING FOR A SEAT IN THE ONTARIO PARLIAMENT. AT FIRST I WAS SHOCKED BECAUSE HIS ENGLISH WAS NOT GOOD ENOUGH, BUT I REALIZED THAT HIS MOTIVATION AND THE EXPOSURE TO POLITICAL CAMPAIGNS MIGHT HELP TO IMPROVE HIS WRITING AND READING SKILLS. OTHERWISE, HE HAD ALL THE SKILLS EVERY POLITICIAN SHOULD HAVE.

Spotlight out on JAMES, *and cross-fade up on* DENIS.

DENIS
(Signing and talking.)

My first reaction to news of Gary running for office was, 'My God, I hope he does it.' Because I was thinking about his feelings and knowing how hard he would work. And if he wasn't successful, what that might do to him. Because to run in any election, the time commitment is incredible and mustering up the support from people, going door to door. I was skeptical. Knowing how much work on the phone there is, keeping people on side and your key people from getting pissed off over some issue and not being able to pick up the phone and calm them down. I was skeptical from that end that it would be possible. I was really worried knowing how much energy he would put into running an election, what might happen to him if he didn't win.

Spotlight out on DENIS *and cross-fade up o*n GARY

GARY
(*reading from a letter.*)

DEAR MEMBERS OF THE YORK EAST NDP RIDING ASSOCIATION, I AM WRITING TO YOU TO ANNOUNCE MY INTENTION TO SEEK THE NDP NOMINATION FOR THE RIDING OF YORK EAST IN THE NEXT PROVINCIAL ELECTION AND REQUEST YOUR SUPPORT. AS YOU MAY HAVE HEARD, I AM THE FIRST DEAF PERSON TO RUN FOR ELECTED OFFICE IN NORTH AMERICA. I AM VERY EXCITED ABOUT THIS CHALLENGE AND LOOK FORWARD TO WORKING WITH YOU AND THE NDP TO MAKE THE ELECTORAL PROCESS MORE ACCESSIBLE TO ALL THOSE WHO HAVE BEEN DENIED IN THE PAST. I AM PERSONALLY INTERESTED IN EDUCATION, EMPLOYMENT EQUITY, TENANT'S RIGHTS, DAY CARE AND THE ENVIRONMENT. I FEEL THAT MY EXPERIENCE AND BACKGROUND WILL MAKE ME AN EXCELLENT REPRESENTATIVE FOR THE PEOPLE OF YORK EAST. IT'S TIME TO CHALLENGE THE RECORD OF THE LIBERAL GOVERNMENT AND TO SHOW THE PEOPLE OF ONTARIO THAT THE NDP IS REALLY THE

PARTY THAT REPRESENTS THEM. I INVITE YOU TO JOIN ME AT THE AUGUST FIRST NOMINATION MEETING. I USE A SIGN LANGUAGE INTERPRETER TO FACILITATE COMMUNICATION SO I WILL HAVE NO PROBLEM COMMUNICATING WITH YOU. TRULY YOURS, GARY MALKOWSKI, YORK EAST RESIDENT.

Spotlight out on GARY *and cross-fade up on* NARRATOR.

NARRATOR

On July 30, 1990 the Liberal provincial government of Ontario called an election to be held on September 6, 1990. At the time, the polls showed that the Liberals led the other parties with 50% support of decided voters. The New Democratic Party had 26% and the Progressive Conservatives had 22%. Two days later, on August First, the York East NDP Riding Association hosted a nomination meeting at the East York Community Center on Pape Avenue in Canada's biggest city, Toronto.

Lights come up full on a meeting hall. GARY *sits down in the front row with a group of friends and supporters that includes* KAREN, DENIS, JUDY, IRIS, PATTY SHORES-HERMANN. *There is also a* REPORTER *with a television* CAMERAMAN *present.*

LES DIGBY
(At podium with DEAN interpreting next to him.)

Good evening, I am Les Digby, president of the York East Riding Association. Welcome to our nomination meeting. As you can see, we have the

TV news media here and they have a 10 p.m. deadline to make the 11 o'clock news. So if we're going to get the coverage we desire, we're going to need to do things quickly. Without any further ado, I hereby announce that the nominations are open for the New Democratic Party candidate for the riding of York East. Are there any nominations?

> TIM WELCH
> (*Rising from the audience.*)

Yes.

> LES DIGBY
> (*Stepping aside.*)

Tim Welch.

> TIM WELCH
> (*At the podium.*)

I've been a member of the NDP for 12 years and I am proud to nominate Gary Malkowski tonight because he is a fighter. York East residents need someone to battle the unscrupulous landlords and speculators who flip buildings and then raise the rents to circumvent rent control legislation. Gary Malkowski will be a very effective Member of Provincial Parliament.

> LES DIGBY
> (*Stepping to the podium as* TIM *departs.*)

Is there a second?

> VOICE FROM THE CROWD

I second the nomination.

LES DIGBY

Are there any other nominations?
>*(No response.)*

Are there any other nominations?
>*(No response.)*

Let the record show that there are no other nominees. All in favor of Gary Malkowski as the NDP candidate for the York East NDP please raise your hand.
>*(Everyone raises a hand goes up.)*

Any opposed?
>*(No opposed.)*

Then it's unanimous and official.
>*(Applause and hand waving.)*

Now, here to speak in support of Gary is leader of the provincial NDP, the honorable Bob Rae.

BOB RAE *rises from the audience and goes to the podium as the crowd applauds and waves their hands.*

BOB RAE

Thank you. Thank you....(*Smiling.*) Well, I've always said that you can tell a party by the company it keeps. Congratulations, Gary. I am delighted and proud that our party is behind this breakthrough: the first deaf candidate in Canada—some say North America. This is further evidence that we are the party of disadvantaged and disenfranchised. The party in power is the party of developers, landlords and big business.
>*(Pause.)*

The Deaf community has made great strides under Gary's leadership. He's made the Liberal government sit up and listen. This is a great

example of how other communities in the province
need to act to affect change in the political process.
I, for one, can't wait to see Gary Malkowski in the
legislature.

(Applause.)

Gary, I need to run off to another nomination
meeting, but I want you to know you are going to
have the full support of the NDP. I brought my
wife and daughters here this evening because the
NDP is making history tonight and I wanted them
to see it. We are very, very proud that Gary has
chosen to become an active member of our party.
And we are very, very proud of the York East
riding.

The crowd applauds and waves hands as **BOB RAE** *comes
to* **GARY. GARY** *stands and they shake hands.* **BOB RAE**
*waves his hands back at the audience, joining them in the
deaf applause.*

JUDY *comes to the podium as* **BOB RAE** *shakes a few
hands and waves at the crowd.*

JUDY

Thank you, Bob.....The next premier of Ontario.
(More applause.)

Hello, everyone. I am Judy Rebick. I am not
speaking tonight as President of the National Action
Committee on the Status of Women, but as a friend
and colleague of Gary's. I want you all to know
that Gary is one of the most gifted leaders I've ever
come across in twenty years of political activity.
He's a fighter. Very determined. One hundred and
fifty percent committed to the people he's leading.
He will bring that commitment to York East. Gary
has never let his ego get in the way of learning how

to do something better. He always asks for feedback after a political meeting or action. Gary is willing to do whatever is necessary, including to change personally to achieve the objective. He has the potential to become a brilliant and great leader.

(More applause.)

Now, Richard Johnston, the retiring M.P.P. from Scarborough would like to say as few words on Gary's behalf.

RICHARD

(Rises from the audience and goes to the podium as JUDY *sits down.)*

Hello, everyone. Two years ago, when Gary and Judy came to my office to discuss the deaf education problems, I was `burnt out and cynical after 11 years in the legislature. They inspired me to assist and I was proud to be apart of the Deaf Ontario Now movement. My only regret is that the Liberal devils didn't pass Bill 112, that would have allowed ASL to be an option in the classroom, just a choice in a deaf child's education. Minister of Education, Sean Conway had promised to take action on the bill in the fall, knowing full well that an election call in the summer would waylay it. This government should be ashamed. Look at York East's current M.P.P., Christine Hart. We have all read about her troubles. Christine is no longer pristine.

(Some small laughter from crowd.)

I apologize to our deaf members for telling a "hearing" joke. This riding can't afford to have a quiet, mousy member afraid to challenge the government, hoping to get into the cabinet and then when she does, doesn't have the kind of morality to be a good cabinet member.

(Pause.)

Gary Malkowski will keep fighting and fighting. He won't take "maybe" for an answer. And if you slam the door on Gary Malkowski in June like they did when the legislature closed without passing Bill 112, then he's going to pop back up as an NDP candidate and shove it in your face in the election!!

> *(Applause, cheers and hand waving.)*

We are going to make history, not tonight, but on September Sixth!

RICHARD *and* GARY *shake hands as* GARY *comes to the podium.*

GARY & DEAN

Wow!! It's a very exciting moment for me. I appreciate all your support. Thank you so much to Richard Johnston. He has been so supportive and important to me and the Deaf Community. He has shared his experience and political skills. I can't wait to get started. This Liberal government has been outstanding for breaking promises. They are all talk and no action. This riding should be proud for nominating the first Deaf person to run for office in North America. So I'm a little unique and we can take advantage of that with the media to get lots of coverage.

(To the REPORTERS.*)*

Would you like to ask me some questions before you go?

REPORTER

Yes! What is going to be your biggest challenge if you join the Ontario Legislature?

GARY & DEAN

The biggest challenge will be for the Ontario government, not for me. They need to make the legislature accessible. They'll need to make a number of accommodations and create legislation, like allowing ASL interpreters on the floor of the house.

REPORTER

Do you consider yourself disabled or handicapped?

GARY & DEAN

No. I consider myself only culturally different. I communicate in a different language and have different values from that culture.

REPORTER #2

Will you require an interpreter the entire time you're working?

GARY & DEAN

Yes. By the way, there's a shortage of qualified ASL interpreters. The government needs to do something about that.

REPORTER #2

Do you read lips?

GARY & DEAN

Yes, but I only get about 20% and that's not enough.

REPORTER #2

How are you going to be able to cope in a very hearing situation in the legislature during debates, when many people are talking at the same time and even hearing reporters can't catch it all?

GARY & DEAN
(*Smiling.*)

Well, maybe there will be a change in the legislature and only one person will be talking at a time. It could be a real improvement, if I were elected.

REPORTERS *and* CROWD *laugh.*

REPORTER #1

Gary, how many deaf people live in the York East riding?

GARY & DEAN

I don't know exactly.

REPORTER #1
(*To* LES DIGBY.)

Do you know Les?

LES

I haven't a clue.

GARY & DEAN

Based on the 1986 census, there's roughly 250,000 deaf people living in Canada, 80,000 in Ontario and 22,000 in Metro Toronto. So there's probably hundreds in this riding of 77,000. But if I am elected I will be dealing with more than just deaf issues. I have my own agenda but I am going to find out what's important to the people of York East.

REPORTER #2

Mr. Malkowski, is your campaign going to be more expensive because you need to have interpreters with you all the time?

GARY & DEAN

Yes, but we have already contacted the Election Expenses Commission to permit interpreter costs to be outside the spending limits for our campaign.

LES DIGBY

Gary, we better let these people go so they can file their stories in time for the news tonight. And we need to get to the most important part of the meeting....

(At the podium.)

Now, we are going to do some substantial fundraising to give Gary the best chance of success. Tim, would you please start passing the hat....

As the TV CAMERAMAN *and* REPORTERS *leave and* TIM *and* LES *gather donations from the crowd,* GARY *and* DEAN *come downstage for a more private conversation.*

GARY

I NEED TO START KNOCKING ON DOORS AND MEETING PEOPLE AND INTRODUCING MYSELF. ARE YOU AVAILABLE TOMORROW AT 10 IN THE MORNING?

DEAN

NO. I AM GOING OUT OF TOWN TOMORROW MORNING.

GARY

OKAY, I WILL SEE IF SHEILA'S AVAILABLE.

DEAN

NO. SHE'S GOING TO.

GARY

GOING WHERE?

DEAN

THERE'S A BIG INTERPRETERS' CONFERENCE IN VANCOUVER STARTING TOMORROW. ALL THE INTERPRETERS I KNOW ARE GOING.

GARY

OH, SHIT! YOU'RE KIDDING?

DEAN

NO!

GARY

WHAT AM I GOING TO DO?

DEAN

WAIT UNTIL WE GET BACK.

GARY

I CAN'T WAIT!

DEAN

LOOKS LIKE YOU ARE ON YOUR OWN.

DEAN *shrugs and walks away.*

GARY
(*To the audience.*)
WHAT HAPPENS NOW?!

Lights out on the meeting room scene. Lights slowly come up on three or four doorways placed around the bare stage. GARY appears on stage wearing two lawn signs, one over his chest and the other over his back. The signs are tied together by twine and read "MALKOWSKI FOR M.P.P. – YORK EAST". The signs are designed in green, white and orange.

With some pamphlets in hand, GARY knocks on the first door. A woman appears, GARY gestures "hello" and points at his sign on his chest and then points to his face. The WOMAN smiles weakly and GARY gives her a pamphlet. She looks at it and then exits into her doorway shaking her head.

GARY moves on to the next house, knocking on the doorway. A senior citizen gentleman comes to the doorway.

SENIOR CITIZEN

Yes?

GARY

Hello.

SENIOR CITIZEN

Hello.

(GARY *points to his sign.*)

What?

(GARY *tries to hand him a pamphlet but he refuses to take it.*)

What the hell...? No, I don't want that....

113

GARY *shrugs and continues on to another doorway.*

SENIOR CITIZEN
They're not home.

GARY *knocks. A dog barks.*

SENIOR CITIZEN
I said they're not home!

GARY *knocks again. A dog continues to bark.*

SENIOR CITIZEN
Are you deaf?! They are not home!

GARY *shrugs and walks away. He catches sight of the old man and waves with a smile. Lights out on the doorways and spotlight up on* GARY.

GARY
I TRIED CAMPAIGNING AND CANVASSING WITHOUT AN INTERPRETER, BUT I FELT LIKE A COMPLETE FOOL. IT WAS A STUPID THING TO DO. IT TURNED PEOPLE OFF BECAUSE I COULDN'T COMMUNICATE WITH THEM. BUT I DIDN'T HAVE A CAMPAIGN MANAGER TO HELP ME. IT WAS TWO WEEKS INTO THE CAMPAIGN BEFORE I GOT MARCIA MCVEA.

MARCIA McVEA
(Spotlight on her.)

That was the norm. It was very typical for candidates to not get a campaign manager until a couple of weeks into the race. When the party assigned me to manage Gary's campaign, they told me he was deaf and I just thought, "Oh, he can't hear." It didn't mean anything more than that to me. They said, "You can understand him when he speaks." That bit of reassurance wasn't quite true. Soon I would learn all about ASL interpreters.

(She laughs.)

At first, I didn't understand how you use them. And no one took time to explain what the rules were. I couldn't understand why they couldn't stuff some envelopes when they weren't interpreting...In fact, I still don't.

(She laughs.)

The Malkowski campaign staff consisted of three paid workers, two canvass organizers and me. We had about thirty volunteers. There were lots of deaf people—many of Gary's friends and some NDP faithful.

Spotlight down to half on MARCIA, *full spot on* KAREN.

KAREN
(In the spotlight.)

I remember once when I was volunteering in the campaign office with two older women. We were stuffing envelopes with literature and Gary and his team of interpreters were going in and out of the office all afternoon long. After a couple of hours, one woman leaned over and said to the other, "I think Mr. Malkowski has lost his voice." I burst out laughing and told them, "No, Gary's deaf. He doesn't speak." They were both stunned and couldn't imagine how he was ever going to succeed.

Spotlight out on KAREN, *back to full on* MARCIA.

MARCIA

There are three steps in a campaign: One, get the message out; two, find out who supports you by going door-to-door; and three, get the vote out on election day. We were getting lots of media coverage because of Gary's uniqueness, but no one seriously thought Gary would win. The Tories held the seat for more than 30 years before the Liberals grabbed it in 1986. The NDP last held York East seat in the 1940's.

(Pause.)

With our limited budget and manpower, we staged a number of splashy events and pizzazz, but it was only smoke and mirrors. We gave the appearance that things were place, but we didn't have the people or the money to follow through.

Spot light up full on GARY.

GARY

AT THE TIME OF THE CAMPAIGN, THE ELECTION FINANCES ACT DID NOT ALLOW FOR CANDIDATES' ACCESSIBILITY COSTS. THERE WAS AN ALLOWANCE FOR COSTS FOR DISABLED VOTERS, BUT NOT FOR DISABLED CANDIDATES. EACH CANDIDATE WAS ALLOWED A BUDGET UP TO $45,000, DEPENDING ON THE NUMBER OF VOTERS IN THE RIDING. I HAD TO CUT

THE BUDGET IN HALF, BECAUSE I HAD TO PAY $20,000 FOR INTERPRETERS, WHICH LEFT INSUFFICIENT FUNDS COMPARED TO THE EXPENDITURES OF NON-DISABLED CANDIDATES.

MARCIA

At the time, I felt good that even if Gary didn't get elected, progress had been made. We were successful in getting the Election Expenses Commission to allow extra expenses incurred by disabled candidates not to fall under the campaign's ceiling for expenses.

GARY

MY INTERPRETERS WERE PAID BUT THEY ALSO VOLUNTEERED A LOT OF THEIR TIME AS WELL. CANVASSING WITH ME IS HARD WORK. I FELT LIKE I KNOCKED ON EVERY DOOR IN THE YORK EAST RIDING AND IT WAS A WONDERFUL EXPERIENCE. I THINK PEOPLE WERE IMPRESSED WITH THE NDP PLATFORM AND I THINK THEY LIKED THE FACT THAT I ADMITTED I DIDN'T HAVE ALL THE ANSWERS. I TOLD PEOPLE I WOULD DO RESEARCH AND LOOK FOR SOLUTIONS.

Spotlights out, and lights up on campaign office. DEAN *joins* GARY *and* MARCIA *in the campaign office.* GARY *puts his campaign signs over shoulders.*

MARCIA

Hey, what are you doing with that?

GARY & DEAN

I'm going canvassing.

MARCIA

But you don't need the signs now that you have an interpreter, right?

GARY & DEAN

Right, but I want to continue wearing the signs. It draws attention, makes me stand out.

MARCIA

Gary, you already stand out, for God's sake. You are the only deaf candidate running for political office that the world has ever seen.

GARY & DEAN

I think people like it when I come to their doors.

MARCIA

Okay, if it makes you happy. Get out of here before I change my mind.

GARY *and* DEAN *rush out.*

MARCIA
(*To the audience.*)

I was dead set against Gary wearing those signs. The central campaign had a fit when they heard, but I told them it made Gary happy and it was better than something else he wanted to do, which was ride a bike around honking a horn. People would have thought we had Harpo Marx running for office.

Lights out on MARCIA *and up on the three doorframes.*
GARY *and* DEAN *ente*r. GARY *knocks on the door. The
same* WOMAN *from the earlier visit, re-appears.*

GARY & DEAN

Hello! I'm Gary Malkowski and I'm running for
Provincial Parliament. I just wanted to stop by and
say hello and ask for your vote.

WOMAN
(*Talking to* DEAN.)

Which one of you is the candidate?

GARY

I AM.

DEAN
(*Pointing.*)

He is. He says, "I am."

WOMAN

Oh. What party are you with?

GARY & DEAN

The New Democratic Party.

WOMAN

Oh. Okay. We usually vote NDP.

GARY & DEAN

Great. Then Bob Rae and I can count on your vote
for September 6?

                    WOMAN
Yes.

                  GARY & DEAN
Thank you. Have a nice day.

                    WOMAN
Thank you.

As the woman disappears, GARY *and* DEAN *move on to the next door way.* GARY *knocks and the* SENIOR CITIZEN *appears.*

                  GARY & DEAN
Hello!

                 SENIOR CITIZEN
Oh, it's you again.

                  GARY & DEAN
Yes, it's me. I brought an interpreter this time so we can communicate better.

                 SENIOR CITIZEN
Why do you need an interpreter? Why don't you get a hearing aid like I have?

                  GARY & DEAN
Hearing aids don't really help me. I was born deaf.

                 SENIOR CITIZEN
Oh, I see.

GARY & DEAN

Tell me something, did you have to pay for your hearing aid?

SENIOR CITIZEN

Sure did. It was expensive, too.

GARY & DEAN

I know. If the NDP wins the election, we'll expand health care services to cover senior citizens and the disabled for expenses like hearing aids.

SENIOR CITIZEN

That would be great. It's hard to make ends meet when you're living on a fixed income and you get hit with a big bill.

GARY & DEAN

Yes, I certainly understand that. I hope you vote for me, Gary Malkowski, on September 6.

SENIOR CITIZEN

Well, I'll think about it.

GARY & DEAN

Thank you. Have a good day.

SENIOR CITIZEN

Thank you.

GARY and DEAN move on to the next house. GARY knocks on the door and a dog starts barking.

DEAN
A BIG DOG IS BARKING.

GARY

DON'T WORRY IT'S NOT GOING TO BITE
YOU.

> (GARY *knocks again.*)

DEAN

> (*As the dog continues to bark wildly.*)

NO ONE'S HOME, LET'S GO.

GARY

> (*As they exit.*)

DON'T BE AFRAID.

DEAN

NO, I'M NOT. I JUST DON'T LIKE BEING
BITTEN BY DOGS...GETTING BITTEN BY A
GOOSE WAS BAD ENOUGH.

They laugh as **DEAN** *crosses down and speaks and signs to the audience.*

DEAN

A couple of days ago, Gary and I arrived at an
outdoor event in Thorncliffe Park and when we got
out of the car in the parking lot we were chased by a
whole flock of Canada geese. We had to run for
our lives. It was scary! I think they found sign
language threatening, just like some hearing people.

GARY

I THINK THOSE WERE CONSERVATIVE
GEESE.

DEAN

HOW DO YOU KNOW?

GARY

ONLY THEIR RIGHT WINGS MOVED.

DEAN *groans as* GARY *laughs and imitates a bird flying with only his right wing moving up and down. The lights go out on them and spotlight up on* MARCIA.

MARCIA

Gary was a good campaigner. He made up for his inexperience with his energy and drive. He nearly ran himself ragged. One day, he came back from canvassing, looking pale. He said, "I think I'm going to faint." So we sat him down, gave him something to eat and drink. And when he was feeling better, I sent him back out there.

(She laughs.)

Spot out on MARCIA *and up on* REPORTER #1.

REPORTER #1

York East Liberal incumbent Christine Hart may have weathered the controversy surrounding her resignation from cabinet, but she's facing a tough battle. Gary Malkowski, a 32-year-old deaf rights activist hopes to win the seat for the NDP and become the first deaf member of the legislature.

Malkowski says there are many issues not being addressed, including tenants' rights, improving senior citizens' lot in life and better facilities for disabled.

Spot out on REPORTER #1 *and up on* MARCIA.

MARCIA

Christine Hart was not a strong campaigner. She and the Liberals seem to think they were a shoe-in. The Conservatives had a novice running in this riding, but they weren't popular because the federal Conservatives with Brian Mulroney as Prime Minister were wildly unpopular. As election day approached, it started to seem as if we might have a chance. A lot of people attend the all candidates' meetings, so there was a good number of undecided voters. Gary held his own in the debates.

Lights up on GARY *behind a podium with* DEAN *standing beside him.*

GARY & DEAN

I won the debates.

MARCIA

I think that's debatable. But you didn't lose, and that was important.

Lights out on MARCIA *and up on* CHRISTINE HART *behind a podium and* GEORGE BRYSON *behind a podium.* DEAN *joins* GARY *behind his podium.*

CHRISTINE HART

...Of my two opponents, there is no question that I have the experience that the voters of York East are looking for in a Member of Provincial Parliament.

GEORGE BRYSON
(With biting sarcasm.)

More experience accepting gifts from lobbyists.

GARY & DEAN

Both Christine and George are right. Experience is important in serving constituents and integrity is also, important, perhaps, even more important than experience.

I believe I am the best candidate because I have experience bringing people together, forming coalitions, and working with the government to make real change. I am honest and hard-working, which my co-workers at the Canadian Hearing Society and my colleagues at the Ontario Association of the Deaf can testify on my behalf.

The "audience" applauds and waves their hands wildly, as lights fade out on the candidates and up on MARCIA *in the campaign office, which is a beehive of activity. People are answering phones and making calls. Deaf supporters are stuffing envelopes and others are making signs.*

MARCIA

On September First, five days before election day, the *Toronto Star* newspaper ran a headline that jolted everyone in Ontario. It read: "NDP ahead of Liberals in latest poll." The NDP had 38% to the Liberals 34%, while the Conservatives had 24%.

GARY & DEAN
(With the newspaper.)

Do you think this means I'm going to win?

MARCIA
(*Laughing.*)

No. It means the party is ahead in the province. You are still a long shot here, Mister. This is still a small "C" conservative riding.

RICHARD
(*Entering the office.*)

Hello! Hello! How are things?

GARY & DEAN

Richard! Did you see the newspaper?

RICHARD

Yes, but you can't believe most of what the media puts out there. Don't get your hopes up. I have said all along that this is probably going to be a two-step process for you. Currently, this is a wonderful platform to get your agenda out there and gain experience. Then after this election, you'll need to follow Queen's Park events for a few years and then run again in the next election. You'll have a great shot of winning a seat then.

GARY & DEAN

I think I'm going to win now! Did you see all the orange, green and white lawn signs with my name on your way over here?

RICHARD

Yes, but that's not something you can rely on. Most voters in this riding don't even have a lawn or a sign. But just keep on doing what you're doing. Visit the elderly homes, have meetings at high-rises, visit all the store fronts on the Danforth and get to know the big shots in the Greek community on Pape Avenue.

GARY & DEAN

I've done that.

MARICA

He's done that. He's a real workhorse.

RICHARD

Well, do it again. Some folks will need a reminder as the Liberals try to turn things around here in the last few days. They're desperate. They'll make all kinds of promises they can't keep. Just keep reminding people what you and the party stand for.

GARY & DEAN

Okay. Thank you for your support.

They shake hands.

RICHARD

My pleasure, Gary. Enjoy these last few days and be proud of yourself, no matter what happens. You've run a good campaign here and made history.

Lights down on the campaign office and a spotlight up on GARY as he steps out of the setting.

GARY
(*To the audience.*)

WHAT I REMEMBER MOST ABOUT SEPTEMBER 6TH, 1990, ELECTION DAY, WAS THE ORANGE NDP LAWN SIGNS WITH MY

NAME ON THEM PLANTED ON NEARLY
EVERY YARD ALONG MORTIMER AVENUE
WHEN I DROVE TO THE CAMPAIGN OFFICE.
IT WAS A LONG DAY. THE CAMPAIGN WAS
OVER AND THE WORKERS AND
VOLUNTEERS WERE MAKING SURE OUR
SUPPORTERS WERE GETTING TO THE
POLLS IN THE EVENING, AFTER THE POLLS
CLOSED WE ALL CONGREGATED AT THE
CAMPAIGN OFFICE. WE SET UP SOME
TELEVISIONS AND WATCHED AS THE
RETURNS CAME IN AND WINNERS WERE
ANNOUNCED. IT WAS VERY EXCITING.
ALL MY DEAF COMMUNITY FRIENDS WERE
THERE. ALL MY COLLEAGUES FROM CHS.
EVERYONE FROM THE RIDING
ASSOCIATION AND THE CAMPAIGN WERE
THERE.

*Lights come up on the campaign office, now packed with
people.* KAREN, JUDY, LOIS, DENIS, PATTY, DEAN,
MARCIA, RICHARD, LES DIGBY, TIM WELCH *and
others are milling about the office chatting and eating. As*
GARY *moves into the scene a group of deaf guys gather
around* GARY, *patting him on the back and teasing him.*

MARCIA
(*To herself, as she watches TV.*)

I can't believe what I'm seeing.....Richard, do you
see this?! The NDP is winning in riding after
riding....

RICHARD

Yes, it's stunning, isn't it?

REPORTER #1
(Either heard through the P.A. or seen on TV screen.)

...And in the hotly challenged race in York East....

MARCIA

Quiet everyone!!!

The office quickly comes to a hush. DEAN interprets the TV audio for GARY and the deaf supporters.

REPORTER #1

....With 10% of the returns in, Liberal incumbent Christine Hart is holding a slim lead over NDP candidate Gary Malkowski, 784 to 650 votes. Conservative candidate George Bryson well back with 511....

The room begins to buzz with excitement again.

GARY
(A little glum.)

I'M LOSING.....

PATTY

BUT YOU'RE CLOSE, THAT'S ONLY TEN PERCENT OF THE VOTES.

MARCIA
(Coming to GARY.)

What's the matter?

GARY & DEAN

I'm behind by 130 votes.

MARCIA

That's nothing. The votes from Leaside are traditionally reported first and that's a very conservative end of the riding. We're fine.

KAREN

Do you really think so?

MARCIA

Yes! Don't worry.

MARCIA *walks away as* KAREN *and friends gather around* GARY *again, urging him "not to worry."*

Lights fade to half on the campaign office and the actors freeze. Spotlight up on the NARRATOR.

NARRATOR

And so, that night with each subsequent news report, Gary Malkowski cut into the incumbent's lead, until finally around nine-thirty that night the Canadian Broadcast Company news reported....

REPORTER #1

We are projecting a winner in the hotly contested Metro Toronto riding of York East....

MARCIA

Quiet everyone!! Here it is!

The room falls silent.

REPORTER #1

With 80% of the returns in, this may be the biggest upset in a night of upsets, we are declaring Gary Malkowski as the winner......

Instant bedlam, as everyone in the office starts to celebrate. GARY jumps straight into the air with his fists clenched. Camera flashes go off. People are hugging, applauding, high-fiving and screaming for joy.

KAREN and GARY embrace and everyone surrounds them, jumping, hooting, hollering, and trying to pat him on the back. Shouts of "We did it!" and "He did it!" are heard and/or seen. As the celebration continues, the lights start to fade on the scene and an image of GARY frozen in time as he jumps in the air with his clenched fists, is projected above it all.

NARRATOR

The final results of the 1990 election in the York East riding were 9,960 votes or 37.5% for Malkowski, 9,177 votes or 35% for the incumbent, and 7,210 votes or 27% for the conservative candidate. That night Bob Rae became premier of Ontario as the New Democratic Party won a majority government with 74 seats to the Liberals 36 and the Conservatives 20. Two weeks later, Gary Malkowski became the first elected culturally deaf person to be sworn into public office.

End of Act Two.

EPILOGUE

The lights come up on a tableau of GARY MALKOWSKI *standing center stage, with one hand on a bible on a podium or desk and one hand in the air, taking the oath of office. He is surrounded by the entire cast. They stand frozen for a few moments. A flash as if from a photographer's camera occurs, and then* GARY *moves down center and speaks to the audience.*

GARY

IT FEELS GREAT TO BE HERE. IT'S A REAL HONOR. I THINK DEAF PEOPLE AND DISABLED PEOPLE AROUND THE WORLD ARE LOOKING TO THIS AS A HISTORICAL MOMENT.

(He bows.)

THANK YOU.

CURTAIN.

About the Author

Richard Medugno, a graduate of UC Irvine's School of Fine Arts, is a playwright and freelance writer who lives in Fremont, California with his wife and two children. Before moving to Northern California, Mr. Medugno resided in East York, Ontario, Canada, where he was a constituent, eyewitness and later a friend of Member of Provincial Parliament, Gary Malkowski. *BIGGER DREAMS* is a stage adaptation of Medugno's own soon-to-be published biography, *DEAF POLITICIAN: The Gary Malkowski Story*. Mr. Medugno is also the author of a number of plays, including *SILENT SALZBURG*, an award-winning drama about a Christian family that goes into hiding in 1940 Austria to protect their deaf son from sterilization by the Nazis.